The Church
and the
Homosexual

John J. McNeill, S.J.

DARTON, LONGMAN & TODD

First Published in Great Britain in 1977
by Darton, Longman and Todd Ltd
85 Gloucester Road,
London SW7 4SU

ISBN 0 232 51370 8

Imprimi Potest
Eamon G. Taylor, S.J.
Provincial
New York Province, Society of Jesus

Printed in Great Britain by litho at
The Anchor Press Ltd and bound by
Wm Brendon & Son Ltd, both of Tiptree, Essex

*I pray that with God's merciful grace
this book may serve the spiritual good
of all who read it.*

Contents

Preface   vii
Introduction: The Need for a Reappraisal   1

PART 1

I   MORAL THEOLOGY AND HOMOSEXUALITY   29
     The Present Situation   29

II   SCRIPTURE AND HOMOSEXUALITY   37
     The Use of Scripture   37
     The Need for a Definition of Homosexuality   39
     The Sodom and Gomorrah Story in Genesis   42
     Problems of Translation   50
     The Interpretation of Romans 1:26   53
     The Old Testament Context   56
     The Creation Account in Genesis   60

III   TRADITION AND HOMOSEXUALITY   67
     The Appeal to Tradition   67
     The Homosexual Interpretation of the Sodom
        Story   68
     The Development of Legal Tradition   75
     The Anomalies of Tradition   83

IV   TRADITION AND HUMAN NATURE   89
     The Influence of Stoicism   89
     Stoicism and the Church Fathers   93
     Aquinas and Stoicism   95
     Homosexual Activity and Procreation   98
     Human Nature and Homosexuality   101
     Human Freedom and Human Sexuality   103

V   THE HUMAN SCIENCES AND HOMOSEXUALITY   109
     The Use of Scientific Data   109

Promiscuity and Homosexuality   111
Psychiatry and Homosexuality   113
The Controversy among Psychiatrists   120

PART 2

VI TOWARD A POSITIVE APPROACH OF MORAL
    THEOLOGY   129
        The Teleological Perspective   130
        The Positive Contribution of the Homosexual
            Community   131
        Homosexuality and the Relation of the Sexes   135
        Homosexuality and Violence   138
        Homosexuality and Human Service   141
        The Role of the Lesbian   143
        The Homosexual and the Church   144

PART 3

VII PASTORAL MINISTRY TO THE HOMOSEXUAL
     COMMUNITY   151
        The Failure of Pastoral Ministry   151
        Personal Ministry to the Individual   154
        The Church and the Reform of Civil Law   156
        The Goal of Heterosexual Adjustment   160
        The Case For and the Case Against Sexual
            Abstinence   164
        Ministry to the Homosexual Community   172
        Moral Norms and the Homosexual   176
        The Positive Role of the Christian Homosexual
            Community   180
        The Accusation of Sexism   184

VIII CONCLUSION: JUSTICE, THE CHURCH, AND
      THE HOMOSEXUAL   187
        Epilogue   193
        Notes   197

Preface

The history of how I came to write this book and what happened in the process of seeking publication will, I believe, be of interest to the reader and shed some light on the difficulty of fostering an intelligent and open discussion on the subject of homosexuality, especially within the Church. As C. A. Tripp observed of society at large, in the chapter on politics and homosexuality in his recent book *The Homosexual Matrix*, there is "a fiercely dangerous set of emotions that has proved itself capable of corrupting every channel of enlightenment and of suppressing information that would ultimately be useful to everyone's understanding of himself and the world around him."[1] A concerted effort was made within certain sectors of the Church to prevent this book from seeing the light of day. But, thank God, the convictions of reasonable, courageous men prevailed, and as a result this book can now be published with an official *imprimi potest*.

The history of my manuscript began when I published a series of three articles entitled "The Christian Male Homosexual" in the *Homiletic and Pastoral Review* in 1970. These articles were well received, and their enthusiastic reception led me to believe that the time was ripe for a full-scale, book-length study of the moral and pastoral issues of homosexuality. A first draft of the book was ready for publication in 1972 and I began my search for a publisher.

On Labor Day weekend in 1973 I gave the keynote speech at the first national convention of Dignity, an organization for Catholic homosexuals. That speech, which represented a summary statement of the manuscript, was subsequently published in the 5 October 1973 issue of the *National Catholic*

---

1. New York: McGraw-Hill, 1975.

Reporter. The response was staggering. Literally hundreds of letters poured into my office, mostly from priests and religious who were attempting to counsel homosexuals, asking advice and inquiring about the manuscript of the forthcoming book. In January of 1974 I had an offer of publication from Sheed and Ward.

Almost simultaneously with the offer of publication I received a notice from my Jesuit superiors that Father General Pedro Arrupe, S.J., had written from Rome ordering me not to publish anything in the popular press and not to address homosexual groups. (At a later date, officials told me that with the appearance of the article in the *National Catholic Reporter*, pressure was brought to bear on Father General by various Roman Congregations to take some action against me in the matter.) I was particularly upset by this prohibition, first because the implication of the letter that the moral debate could be carried on outside the notice of the public media and exclusively on a peer-group level seemed to me to be totally impracticable; and secondly because I was convinced that it was only through open discussion, with the Catholic homosexual community participating as an equal partner, that any real advance could be made in the Church's moral understanding of homosexuality and consequent pastoral practice.

In the meantime, while participating in an all-day seminar on Christian sexuality sponsored by the Newark diocese of the Episcopal Church, I was asked a question concerning homosexual marriages. I was erroneously reported in a church magazine, the *Living Church*, as approving "the liturgical solemnification of homosexual marriages." When this report reached Rome, pressure was again brought to bear on Father General. A second letter arrived in which I was forbidden to speak, publish, or teach anything on the question of homosexuality until a commission of theologians had examined my teaching.

A commission was set up, and reports were received from

my fellow Jesuit theologians Avery Dulles, Richard McCormick, Richard Roach, and Robert Springer. Charles Curran of
Catholic University and an outstanding biblical scholar who
has asked to remain anonymous also did reports. Although they
did not necessarily agree with my arguments and conclusions,
yet, I understand, a majority of the commission reported that
they found the manuscript a serious and scholarly work worthy
of publication. Several felt strongly that there should be a
public debate on all the issues involved and that my manuscript would be an important contribution to that debate. One
man even urged as a matter of principle that I should publish
the book without submitting it to any form of prior censor-
ship.

The commission's report was forwarded to Father Arrupe
in Rome. He responded in April 1974, saying he was grateful
for the report of the commission but felt that a further step
was needed. Since circumstances had focused personal responsibility on him to stress the need for me to be sensitive
to the traditional norm of morality in my treatment of homosexual conduct, he requested that I forward a copy of my
manuscript to Rome, so that he could review it personally.

After waiting five months for an answer from Rome, I found
out that the manuscript never reached the Father General's
desk, but was lost in a secretary's desk drawer. I was then
told that I should revise the manuscript in the light of the
criticism received from the commission and send a second,
revised version to Rome. After various delays a final revised
copy of the manuscript was sent to Rome in 1975. A reply was
finally received in October. In his reply Father Arrupe turned
over authority to give a "permission to publish" to the
Provincial of the New York Province of the Society of Jesus.
He stated that he would not object to publication granted
that certain suggestions and guidelines be accepted and followed. Among the guidelines suggested was that another

biblical scholar be consulted. In fulfillment of that request, I sent the manuscript to Walter Thompson, S.J., of the Jesuit School of Theology in Chicago.

Father General also requested, among other things, that I make clear where my manuscript differs from the traditional teaching of the Church. After some negotiations with Father Eamon Taylor, S.J., the New York provincial, I made the additions and corrections suggested. The *imprimi potest* was important to me, first of all, because it is my hope that this book will help foster an all-out discussion of the Church's moral understanding and pastoral practice concerning the homosexual. Secondly, I particularly want to reach, and open up new, hopeful possibilities for, all those Catholic homosexuals who are struggling to put together their dual identities as Catholics and as homosexuals. Therefore it was important to me that the book should be accepted into the mainstream of Catholic debate and reflection.

The appearance of the document from the Sacred Congregation for the Doctrine of the Faith, "Declaration on Certain Questions Concerning Sexual Ethics," in January 1976, called into question once again the granting of permission to publish. I informed my superiors how I would respond to the Declaration in my book and was delighted to receive a letter from the provincial, Father Eamon G. Taylor, S.J., on 28 January 1976, saying: ". . . in my opinion the adjustments you have made in your manuscript in accordance with the agreements reached in our conversation of November 10 are responsive to the recommendations of Fr. General's letter of September 19, and . . . as a result, I am happy to be able to grant the *imprimi potest*, as of this date."

It is important for the reader to understand what is implied in the granting of an ecclesiastical *imprimi potest*, i.e. permission to publish, by my religious superiors and what is not implied. First, the authorities that grant the permission in no way commit themselves as agreeing or disagreeing with the content of the book. Rather, all that is implied is that authorities have assured that the book is a prudent work that meets the standards of scholarship for publication of a book on a controversial moral topic. Secondly, the "permission to publish" in no way implies that the conclusions stated in this book are accepted by the Catholic Church as part of its official teaching; only the Pope and the Bishops have the authority to teach officially in the name of the Church.

Consequently, the conclusions arrived at in this book are my personal opinions and their only authority is the value of the reasoning and evidence that I can bring to support them and the confirmation they find in the reader's experience and observations.

I hasten to assure my readers that at no point have I been asked to change or in any way alter my insights or convictions in order to receive official permission to publish. On the contrary, after receiving the critical comments of the various readers, I have been able to strengthen the manuscript and sharpen my position, with the result that the book is, I believe, a much better book.

I especially want to thank all those who generously and courageously supported me through these years of patience and trial, especially Robert J. O'Connell, S.J., who acted as my intermediary with Rome, and Robert Springer, S.J., who was a particularly valued consultant and friend; also Robert Carter, S.J., and the members of the New York Chapter of Dignity who prayed, sorrowed, and rejoiced with me as we went through the ups-and-downs of seeking permission from the Church to publish.

15 January 1976
Crossroads of Reflection and Action,
New York, N.Y.

Introduction
The Need for a Reappraisal

The purpose of this introduction is to indicate both the scope and the limits of this moral and pastoral study concerning the homosexual. The first question that must be posed is: What is the need of a reappraisal of the position of traditional moral theology on the question of homosexuality within the Roman Catholic Community at this time? That need has become evident in recent years to many Roman Catholic priests and laymen engaged in pastoral counseling. They have become progressively aware that the two exclusive aims of traditional pastoral counseling—conversion to a heterosexual orientation or total abstinence from all sexual expression—are no longer practical pastoral aims in a majority of the cases with which they deal.[1] Both from their personal experience as counselors and from available scientific evidence they have come to the conclusion that heterosexual adjustment is a practical and successful aim of counseling only in a minority of cases involving basic homosexual psychic orientation. Further, total and unending sexual abstinence attained without severe emotional disorders, and even mental breakdowns, is a practical and successful goal of counseling again only in a minority of cases.

1

The result of adhering to these exclusive goals has been that many Catholic homosexuals, even a majority, find themselves faced with a terrible dilemma: either to continue their relationship with the Church at the price of being cut off from any deep human relationship and deprived of their potentialities for growth and development in their personal self-identity—not to mention their agonies of guilt, remorse, self-hatred, and potential emotional breakdown when they fail to achieve the accepted goals—or to seek their personal growth by means of a homosexual relationship, only at the price of cutting themselves off from the Church community and its sacramental life, with all the attendant guilt and emotional stress which such a separation involves. When a majority of confessors and counselors find that the traditional guidelines are no longer adequate but, on the contrary, frequently lead to serious harm and destruction for their penitents or patients, the need for a basic critical reexamination of those guidelines should be obvious.

Not only those engaged in pastoral work and counseling but the general public as well has come to a new awareness and a new understanding of the homosexual. In the past the inadequacies of the traditional ways of dealing with the homosexual were hidden from the public view by a virtual conspiracy of silence. Homosexuality was "the sin whose name should not be mentioned." But, thank God, that prejudicial silence has been broken. As the Dutch Cathechism remarks, it was that silence and the absence of any open discussion which allowed prejudice and unfounded fears to flourish, often leading to serious persecutions and injustices.[2]

A brief summary of some of the articles appearing in Catholic publications in the past few years will help give a clearer idea of this remarkable change. As noted in my Preface, in 1970 I published a series of three articles entitled "The Christian Male Homosexual" in the July, August, and September issues of the *Homiletic and Pastoral Review*. These articles, resulting from years of counseling experience and scholarly research, proposed a long overdue change in the pastoral approach to the homosexual, designed to correct social injustices and indignities suffered by homosexuals and stressing that they too are children of Christ's redeeming love. The first article attacked stereotypes and popular misunderstandings concerning the homosexual. The second article dealt with the inadequacies of the two traditional pastoral aims in counseling homosexuals—conversion to heterosexuality and total abstinence from all sexual activity. The third article began a process of ethico-moral reevaluation suggesting that perhaps, within their context and under certain circumstances, homosexual relations could be objectively accepted as a lesser evil than promiscuity, etc., and thus be subjectively acceptable to those in such circumstances as morally good. The enthusiastic response from literally hundreds of priests and religious who wrote seeking further information and urging me to do further research and writing in this field made it clear to me that there was a widespread felt need for this type of reevaluation.

In 1971 Joseph McCaffrey's article "Homosexuality, Aquinas and the Church" in the *Catholic World* made the point that the Church's attitude toward the homosexual had remained basically the same since St. Thomas wrote in the twelve hundreds.[3] McCaffrey questioned whether St. Thomas's understanding of both human nature and human sexuality in general as well as his understanding, or lack thereof, of homosexuality could possibly continue to serve as the basis of moral evaluation today. Father Henry Fahrens, in his article "A Christian Response to Homosexuals" in the September 1972 issue of the *U.S. Catholic*, bore witness from his own and other priests' counseling experience to the inadequacies of the Church's pastoral policies, calling those policies "brutal, self-righteous, prejudicial and un-Christian." Fr. Fahrens called on the Church to be ready to recognize homosexual relations and went so far as to recommend "a witness of the Church to the celebration of love between two people of the same sex."

Commonweal was the next Catholic publication to turn to the issue of homosexuality. The 6 April 1973 issue devoted two major articles and an editorial to the question. The editorial urged the Church to support civil rights legislation for the homosexual and observed that "some Catholic moralists have cautiously argued in professional journals that under certain circumstances which may differ with each individual a Catholic homosexual can enter an active homosexual relationship and still receive the sacraments and lead a life of sexual love which does not necessarily separate him from the love of God."[4] Tom Driver, in his article "Homosexuality: The Contemporary and Christian Contexts," takes the position that appears to be quite generally accepted among Protestant moralists, namely, that "the forms of sexual love do not matter when compared to the dignity of persons and their capacity for trust and love." The Gay Liberation Movement, Driver contends, has raised homosexuality to the level of political consciousness. As a result, we can no longer deal with it as if it were merely a psychological problem or a question of private morality; rather, it is now a question of public policy. "The movement should have our thanks if it causes us to reconsider the policies of marriage, and most of all, if it helps us to see that sexual plurality is the very scene and stage upon which are played out the dramas of love."

Peter Fink, S.J., in the same issue proposed what he called "A Pastoral Hypothesis." He points out that pastoral activity cannot be left in abeyance until complex theological questions are resolved with total clarity. In fact, pastoral activity itself is the source of essential data needed for theological reflection. Fink's hypothesis is that the Church should explore the possibility that homosexual love is a valid form of human love, and, consequently, can also mediate God's loving presence. In the absence of any definitive condemnation of all homosexual activity a priori, it is a valid theological method, Fink argues, to explore this hypothesis and judge its validity on the basis of its consequences. "If homosexual love is sinful this will show itself as destructive of the human and disruptive of man's relation with God." In counseling, the Church should take the gay couple and their attempt at a love union with radical seriousness. "All I ask here is that the Church employ all its resources in an honest effort to lead gay people to love, to the human and to God *through* their homosexuality."

Over Labor Day weekend in 1973 the first national convention of Dignity was held in Los Angeles. I was invited to be the keynote speaker. In my speech I summarized all the evidence in favor of a moral reevaluation of homosexual relations. In its 5 October 1973 issue the *National Catholic Reporter* published my speech and commented in its editorial that there is a growing evidence that it is time for the Church to reexamine its attitude toward the homosexual.[5] What is needed, according to the editor, is "that the Church, individually and corporately, publicly and privately, should sit down with homosexuals and talk in an atmosphere characterized by enlightenment and compassion, not ignorance and invective."

The next major publication occurred again in *Commonweal*. In the 15 February 1974 issue, Gregory Baum in his article "Catholic Homosexuals" saw the affirmation of Gay Catholicism in the form of their organization Dignity as raising many theological questions. The first has to do with the argument traditionally brought against homosexual activity, that based on so-called human nature. We are much more aware today that what was accepted in the past as human nature is a human creation and frequently contains dehumanizing elements which call for theological criticism. Are the prohibitions against homosexuality, Baum asks, "a legitimation of the inherited social structures which assign men and women definitive and unequal places?" Theologians seeing the collective crimes and violence inflicted on homosexual men and women begin to suspect that the traditional arguments against homosexuality are based not so much on a sound concept of nature as on a refusal to take a close look at the foundations of our culture. The crucial moral question, Baum feels, is whether homosexuality is open to mutuality. Is the homosexual orientation capable of grounding friendship that enables the partners to grow and become more human? If the answer is yes, then the task of Catholic homosexuals is to acknowledge themselves as such before God, accept their sexual inclination as an aspect of their calling, and explore the meaning of this inclination for Christian life. This, Baum claims, is the position adopted by Dignity. Dignity holds that it is the call of the Catholic homosexual to affirm his or her sexual orientation in faith, to regard themselves as equal members of the believing community, and to express their sexuality in a manner consonant with Christ's teaching of love.

Homosexual men and women, Baum claims, are in greater need of self-knowledge and personal wisdom than other people. In our culture gay people are often the wounded, and they must wrestle with themselves before the freedom to love and to forget themselves becomes accessible to them. But to whom are they to go? If gay people will ever find guidelines to heal themselves of the wounds that lead to hostility and self-hatred, it will be a wisdom generated within the homosexual community itself. Dignity trusts that the guidance granted by the Spirit within the Christian community will lead to greater insight into unresolved questions. Baum believes it is not likely that the Catholic Church is about to change its traditional teaching, namely, that all homosexual activity, no matter what the circumstances, is sinful. Therefore he

thought it would be a mistake for Dignity to make an appeal
to the Catholic hierarchy for special recognition. Rather, Baum
proposes what he terms a realistic strategy: "to create a mod-
erate and well-founded minority position in the Catholic
Church which would be a help to vast numbers of gay
people at this time, collect more pastoral experience and
continue theological reflection."

Gregory Baum's prediction proved prophetic. Dignity's letter addressed to the Bishops of the United States from its
first national convention, appealing for dialogue, went un-
heeded for the most part. In its place the Bishops' Committee
on Pastoral Research and Practice issued a fifteen-page article:
"Principles to Guide Confessors in Questions of Homosexuality." The principles enunciated in the guidelines are basically
a repetition of the Church's traditional stand concerning homosexuality. Homosexuality is seen as contrary not only to the
procreative purpose of human sexuality, "but also to the other
principle, which is to express mutual love between husband
and wife." The guidelines also claim that homosexual activity
is clearly condemned in Scripture, especially in Paul's Epistle
to the Romans. The document summarizes various theories as
to the cause of homosexuality, with the presumption that it
represents a pathological condition. Despite its obvious limitations, some writers praised the guidelines as the first document
originating from Church authorities in recent times to give
explicit attention to the homosexual question. The most important new element in the text is the encouragement of
sexually non-active homosexual friendships. Traditionally many
moralists argued that homosexuals should avoid such friendships because they could be an "occasion of sin." However,
the Bishops' statement argues that "other elements in his
[the homosexual's] plan of life and spiritual direction can
temper this danger which is justified considering his need for
deep human relationships, and the good which will come from

them in the future." However, the document insists, if a homosexual friendship begins to involve regular overt sexual activity, then the homosexual must be admonished to break off
the relationship, with the sanction for refusal to do so the
refusal of absolution.

The primary source of the Bishops' guidelines is to be found
in the writings of John Harvey.[6] Father Harvey is a pioneer
in the area of moral studies and research concerning homosexuality. He takes a strongly negative view on homosexual
relationships, believing them to be contrary to God's will as
revealed in Scripture and, from his own pastoral experience,
humanly destructive. Father Harvey has sought the financial
assistance of the American Bishops to open an institution for
homosexual priests where they could receive special psychological and spiritual assistance.

At its annual meeting in Denver in 1972, the National
Federation of Priests' Councils passed a resolution dealing with
ministry to the homosexual community. The Federation noted
that "the Church's concern for and ministry to the homosexual community is practically invisible and, therefore, non-
existent in the United States." Consequently, the Federation
voted to establish a task force to develop a model for a
Christian ministry to the homosexual community. That model
was developed by a Gay ministry task force which the Justice
and Peace Commission of the Salvatorian Fathers established
in 1972. A thirty-eight-page set of guidelines, entitled "A Model
for Ministry to the Homosexual Community," was presented
to the Executive Committee of the National Federation of
Priests' Councils to be submitted to the delegates for a vote
in the 1974 national convention. The guidelines called for full
participation of homosexuals in the Eucharist and directed that
confessions of homosexuals who have accepted their condition
and are comfortable with it should not center on the fact of
homosexuality but on whether the individual is living up to

"the demands of the Christian faith and conversion *as a homosexual.*"

At that convention the Executive Board of the National Federation refused to present the guidelines for a vote by the membership on the grounds that they were "not complete enough." President Reid Mayo referred to a report by Charles Curran to the effect that the guidelines made the assumption that "there is nothing wrong with homosexual acts per se and that there is no difference between homosexuality and heterosexuality." Curran felt that many theological issues which still remained to be decided among theologians were assumed resolved in the guidelines. Consequently, in place of a vote on the guidelines, the National Federation of Priests' Councils voted unanimously for "a development of the theology of homosexuality." This book is conceived precisely as an effort to make a contribution to that development.

Another circumstance which calls for a reappraisal of the traditional moral position of the Church is the fact that the homosexual community itself has evolved a new self-awareness and a new militancy. Homosexuals in large numbers are no longer content to suffer prejudice and injustice passively; they have grouped together and formed organizations to promote their own sense of self-pride and heal the deep wounds left by their status as a persecuted minority, as well as to promote their own legal and political rights. Perhaps for the first time in history self-accepting homosexuals have emerged as a political force, as the presence of their spokesmen at the 1972 Democratic National Convention gave witness.

This new self-awareness and militancy is not limited, however, to the social and political order; there is a new consciousness and a new militancy among believing homosexuals who are active members of the various Churches. The recent emergence of the Metropolitan Community Church as an interim Christian community for those homosexuals who are not accepted in the other Churches is an example of this. Homosexuals from a Roman Catholic background have also begun to group together in organizations such as Dignity. These homosexuals wish to remain faithful and actively participating members of their Church. But they will no longer accept without challenge the Church's traditional teaching and practice in their regard. They insist on being dealt with as a group, and no longer as isolated individuals; they insist on their right to be represented and to contribute from their collective knowledge and experience to a reappraisal of the Church's traditional pastoral treatment of them. They are anxious to contribute to the task of separating the wheat from the chaff; that is, the real implications of Christian faith and morals concerning their life-style from the traditional customs and prejudices which, as they see it, an often all-too-human heterosexual Church community has imposed on them. For they feel that this Church tradition owes its origin more to prejudice and misunderstanding than to the true implications of Christian faith.

The Church's traditional pastoral position concerning homosexuals was, however, by no means a purely arbitrary stance. It had its foundation in the Church's understanding of the sources of revelation, both Scripture and tradition, and in the traditional interpretation of these sources insofar as they can contribute to the formation of a theological understanding of human sexuality. It had its foundation also in the "natural law" tradition of moral philosophy and moral theology espoused by the Church. Consequently, the Church cannot in good conscience change its pastoral position in such a way that its practice would be in violation of its understanding of both revelation and theology.

The magisterium's most recent pronouncement dealing with homosexuality was issued by the Sacred Congregation for the Doctrine of the Faith on 15 January 1976. The document, entitled "Declaration on Certain Questions Concerning Sexual Ethics," is to my knowledge the first official Church document which deals, among other questions, with the pastoral and moral issues concerning homosexuality. The Declaration is an important document of serious ecclesiastical authority and, as such, it merits a respectful and serious hearing on the part of all who recognize that authority. Although the Declaration is an authoritative pronouncement on what the official teaching of the institutional Church is at this moment in time, it is not, however, an infallible teaching. Its importance is based on extrinsic authority rather than intrinsic argument. There is no effort to present evidence, nor is there any indication of sources, but only a series of authoritative declarations. Consequently it does not simply close the door to all further discussion of the question on the part of competent scholars in the manner of competent scholarship.

Dealing with the moral questions concerning homosexuality, the Declaration speaks of those "who, basing themselves on observations in the psychological order, have begun to judge indulgently, or even to excuse completely, homosexual relations between certain people." The Declaration is the first Church document to grant the legitimacy of the distinction—so important, as we shall see, for moral evaluation—between those who indulge in homosexual activities and those who share in a permanent homosexual condition. Although it grants the validity of the distinction, it does not explore its implications for moral judgment. The document accepts the opinion, rejected by the American Psychiatric Association, that a permanent homosexual psychological condition is "pathological."

In regard to constitutional homosexuals, the document notes: "Some people conclude that their tendency is so natural that it justifies in their case homosexual relations within a sincere communion of life and love analogous to marriage insofar as such homosexuals feel incapable of enduring a solitary life."

It then goes on to insist on pastoral compassion and understanding in dealing with such homosexuals: "[They] must be
treated with understanding and sustained in the hope of overcoming their personal difficulties and their inability to fit into
society." Further, because "in sins of the sexual order . . . it
more easily happens that free consent is not fully given," the
document calls for "prudence" in judging culpability of homosexuals. However, the Declaration is quite clear that "no
pastoral method can be employed which would give moral
justification to these acts on grounds that they would be
consonant with the condition of such people."

Consequently, the authors of the Declaration find themselves
in the dilemma of denying the pastor what, in the opinion
of many, would be the only realistic means of truly helping
the homosexual to overcome his or her difficulty and to fit
into society. As the editors of the *Tablet*, the Catholic newspaper of the Brooklyn diocese, noted in the issue of 22 January
1976:

> To recommend overcoming the incurable is to counsel the impos-
> sible, and it is precisely because of the frustration of such a situa-
> tion that moral theologians are exploring other pastoral solutions.
> The pastoral sensitivity recommended by the Declaration might
> lead to an understanding ministry to such persons, but there must
> also be some deeper inquiry into the nature of the moral condi-
> tion itself.

Why do the authors of the Declaration place themselves in
this dilemma? They make quite clear in the Declaration that
they do not see their pastoral conclusion as arbitrary; rather,
they see it as necessitated by their understanding of sacred
Scripture and of tradition. In sacred Scripture, the document
states, "they [homosexual relations] are condemned as a serious depravity and even presented as the sad consequence of
rejecting God." The document does note that Scripture does
not permit us to conclude that all those who are homosexuals

are personally responsible. However, it nevertheless concludes that the Scriptures "attest to the fact that homosexual acts are intrinsically disordered and can in no way be approved of."

The second argument is based on a certain understanding of moral philosophy and theology, namely that all homosexual acts in the objective moral order "lack an essential and indispensable finality." The basic question here is one of understanding what is the God-given nature and meaning of human sexuality as such. The Church has traditionally held that the only context which can give moral meaning to human sexuality according to God's will is "a relationship which realizes the full sense of mutual self-giving and human procreation in the context of true love."

I am fully in sympathy with the Congregation's concern to preserve moral and human values in the realm of human sexuality. The Church must carry out its divinely appointed task of searching out the context in which human sexual activity is conformed to the will of God and the spirit of Christ. Further, I remind my readers once again that I am not the magisterium; nor do I have the authority to speak in the name of the Church. However, I can speak on this subject with some authority. I am a qualified and accredited theologian and an expert in the field of sexual ethics. I have spent many years studying, counseling, and working with the Catholic homosexual community. My opinions have been shared with my colleagues and revised to meet their legitimate criticisms. The value of what I have to say is not based on extrinsic authority but on the value of the reasoning and evidence that I can bring to bear.

It is my opinion, which I will try to demonstrate in this book, that the limitations on pastoral practice imposed once again by the Declaration will be destructive of the values the document wishes to preserve and will continue to prove

humanly destructive of the majority of Catholic homosexuals
who attempt to live according to its directives. In the words,
once again, of the editors of the *Tablet:* "We are deeply committed to the right and duty of ecclesiastical authority to teach
the truth, but not to the presumption that ecclesiastical authority can create the truth."

Consequently, the Declaration makes quite clear that before
there can be any authentic change in pastoral practice, there
must first be a critical reappraisal of the sources of traditional
practice both in moral philosophy and moral theology. Such
a critical reappraisal becomes even more necessary and urgent
in the light of the new methodologies in both biblical studies
and moral theology and new data arising especially from the
human sciences such as psychology and sociology. By applying
the new methodologies and taking into consideration the new
data, many moral theologians have come to the conclusion that
many of the basic certitudes of the past which served as the
foundation and justification of pastoral practice regarding
homosexuality can and should be open to critical reexamination.

First of all there is an urgent need to apply the new methodologies of biblical scholarship to scriptural data. The primary
source of the traditional condemnation of homosexual activity
as contrary to the divine will has been the interpretation of
certain texts both in the Old and New Testaments which have
been understood as dealing with this subject. Unfortunately,
in using Scripture to deal with homosexuality many still use
a text-picking approach, but biblical scholarship has advanced
beyond this approach in most other areas. There is general
recognition that to get at the true message of Scripture one
must use advanced linguistic tools; one must consider individual texts in their larger context; one must also consider the
cultural and historical circumstances of the time. As a result,
a new understanding of the biblical treatment of human

sexuality in general seems to be emerging among biblical scholars; they appear to be moving toward the realization that Scripture does indeed teach a "personalist" understanding of human sexuality over against the legalist tradition based in natural law.

As I note in this study, there has been surprisingly little scholarly biblical work dealing with homosexuality. However, I have attempted to gather together the results of such studies as have been made. These studies tend to cast serious doubt on the claim that one can find a clear condemnation of all homosexual activity as such, independent of circumstances, in Scripture, or that one can find a clear revelation of God's will which is applicable to the situation of most homosexuals as we understand the situation today.

With regard to the treatment of the biblical material, a special word of gratitude should go to Dr. John Boswell of Yale University. It was while reading his brilliant scholarly reflections, as yet unpublished, dealing with the loci in the epistles of St. Paul supposedly concerned with homosexuality that I first became aware that the traditional scriptural basis for the condemnation of homosexual acts as contrary to the revealed will of God was open to serious question. A special debt of gratitude is due also to D. Sherwin Bailey, whose classic work *Homosexuality in the Western Christian Tradition* still remains the outstanding scholarly work on the subject. I have drawn heavily upon it. Bailey's treatment of the Old Testament passages, especially the Sodom and Gomorrah story in Genesis, first opened my eyes to the fact that the sin of Sodom and Gomorrah was understood by many biblical scholars to be not homosexuality but inhospitality to the stranger. Peter Ellis's book *The Yahwist: The Bible's First Theologian* provided essential information on the Yahwist's persistent theme of ridiculing pagan fertility worship, which helps to put the sexual elements of the Sodom and Gomorrah story into perspective. John McKenzie's book *The World of the Judges* threw light on the parallel passage, the Crime of Gibeah, in Judges. T. C. DeKruijf's *The Bible on Sexuality* provided me with a key to the understanding of the difference in the treatment of human sexuality in the Old and New Testaments. And finally a special word of thanks belongs to Herman van de Spijker, whose work *Die Gleichgeschlechlicke Zuneigung* provided a basically confirmatory analysis of biblical passages.

Also I wish to thank the two biblical scholars who took the time to read over and criticize my manuscript and give me the help of their specialized knowledge. The first, who prefers to remain unnamed, gave me invaluable help with the Old Testament materials. The second, Father Walter Thompson, S.J., whose special studies on the Pauline aspects of the question made him a particularly competent reader, gave me important support in my confrontation with critics. I would like to quote from his critical report:

> I find your treatment of the biblical data judicious and responsible. You clearly disclaim credentials as a biblical scholar and state your dependence on the work of specialists. But within that limitation your selection and arrangement of materials is well-ordered and clear. You obviously have a sense of how an argument from Scripture about a current issue is to be developed. . . . Concerning methodological issues I could not agree more with your assessment of the impact of recent biblical studies in the Church on both dogmatic positions and moral/pastoral questions. . . . Consensus among theologians is not a matter of counting heads. It is a question of those who have understood and made operative in their theology the developments in biblical studies and those who have not.

I make no pretense to be a biblical scholar; I have attempted to gather together the results of the best scholarship concerning those passages in the Old and New Testaments traditionally understood as dealing with homosexuality. My hope is that this summary treatment I give the subject may inspire qualified biblical scholars to undertake a much more thorough study.

When we look at tradition, we find that tradition in turn relies both on a questionable use of Scripture and on a relatively unexamined cultural inheritance. The only new element which enters the picture is the use of "natural law" tradition in scholastic philosophy to buttress the conclusions originally derived from Scripture and cultural practice. As in many other areas of moral philosophy, the advances made in philosophical anthropology, where the human is understood along dynamic lines of self-creative freedom rather than static essence, serve as a basis for a critical reexamination of the traditional condemnation of homosexuality derived from the natural law approach of the Scholastics. We are much more aware today of the extent to which human sexual orientation is the result of a free cultural adaptation rather than biological instinct. The emphasis in ethics concerns a search for ideal goals which should serve as guide and norm for that free cultural development. Sexual ethics in general places a much greater stress on the interpersonal dimension as the proper context within which sexual behavior can be and must be ethically evaluated. Greater stress must be placed on the actual situation of the parties involved. Once all these factors are taken into consideration, the traditional treatment of homosexuality in philosophical ethics appears seriously inadequate.

To avoid possible misunderstandings I would like to call to the attention of my readers the philosophical background from which I approach moral issues in general and sexual morality in particular. It will become evident quickly to the discerning reader that I am not following the classical "natural law" philosophy. Rather, I consider myself a disciple of the great French Catholic philosopher Maurice Blondel, whose philosophy of action was one of the principal sources of

Teilhard de Chardin's thought and played an essential role
in the thinking of many of the periti at the Second Vatican
Council.

In my book *The Blondelian Synthesis*, I discussed Blondel's
fundamental personalist framework for moral evaluation in
the chapter entitled "The Problem of Interpersonality."[7] I
evolved a Blondelian methodology for moral decision making
in a paper entitled "Necessary Structures of Freedom," presented to the Jesuit Philosophical Association,[8] and again from
a different perspective in my paper entitled "Freedom of
Conscience in Theological Perspective," presented to a pastoral
psychology symposium at Fordham University in 1971.[9] I
further developed my ideas on freedom, person, and nature
in an article in a special *Theological Studies* issue on moral
problems in genetics: "Human Freedom and the Future."[10]
Finally, I applied that methodology and its insights to sexual
morality in general in a two-part article, "Joseph Fletcher on
Sexual Behavior: A Critical Comment," in the April and May
1969 issues of the *Homiletic and Pastoral Review*.[11]

There have also been significant changes in the approach
of moral theology to sexual ethics in general. Under the influence of recent psychological insights there has been a
movement away from the act-centered methodology of the
past toward an orientation-centered methodology. As O'Neil
and Donovan note in their recent book *Sexuality and Moral
Responsibility*, the moral quality of sexual activity cannot
be judged from the isolated act; rather it involves "a responsible orientation toward growth and reconciliation."[12] Therefore,
the question must be posed: Can homosexual activities within
the context of a homosexual interpersonal relationship represent a responsible orientation toward growth and reconciliation? Another change which must be taken into consideration.
is the recent emphasis on the coequality of the ends of
sexuality, procreation and mutual support and fulfillment.

As long as procreation was held as the primary aim of all legitimate sexual activity, it was relatively easy to condemn homosexual activity, since it necessarily contradicted that primary aim. It is interesting to note that during the recent birth-control controversy many traditional moralists resisted any effort to challenge that primacy on the grounds that it would tend to undermine the Church's traditional position concerning homosexual activities. The question must now be posed: If a homosexual relationship can achieve the coequal aim of mutual support and fulfillment, is it morally acceptable?

Once again, there certainly is a need for a definitive work on the development of the Church's tradition concerning homosexuality, a work along the lines of Noonan's classical study of contraception and Callahan's study of abortion. The best that can be done in this book is to point out those aspects of tradition concerning homosexuality which are open to critical reexamination owing to the various changes we have noted. It is my hope, once again, that this study may inspire competent scholars to undertake such a work.

Finally, we must consider the enormous amount of new, significant data derived from the human sciences such as psychology, psychiatry, sociology, anthropology, and comparative cultural studies. This data has provided the moralist with an understanding of human sexuality—its etiology, development, cultural dependency, etc.—which calls into question many of the implicit assumptions of the past. One factor which tends to confirm moral theologians in upholding the traditional condemnation of homosexuality is the position of a prevalent school of psychiatrists that homosexuality is an abnormal form of sexual development and constitutes mental illness. However, many prominent psychiatrists have recently challenged their colleagues on this point. In fact, by a unanimous decision the trustees of the American Psychiatric Association have voted to remove homosexuality from the list of mental illnesses, and a majority vote of the membership upheld that decision of the board of trustees. Contrary to traditional belief, several recent studies have revealed the presence in society of many healthy, well-adjusted, and productive people living in stable and happy homosexual relationships. The presence of these relatively happy and whole people in stable relationships that are homosexual exposes the weak epistemological basis of much previous moral evaluation, since it was based on incomplete and inaccurate data.[13]

All efforts in the past to establish a definitive etiological explanation of homosexuality in terms of either constitutional or environmental factors have run into serious difficulties. The result has been controversy and disagreement among psychologists and psychiatrists concerning the etiology, status in terms of mental health, and proper treatment for homosexuals. Some moralists have tended to accept the disputed conclusions of one or another school of psychologists and psychiatrists. Still others have manifested a tendency to make an unjustified transition from supposed psychological data to a moral conclusion. Because, for example, the homosexual was supposedly deprived of proper parental relations in early childhood (psychological), therefore he must work to overcome his homosexuality and become heterosexual (moral). I have attempted to summarize these recent developments in psychology and psychiatry which call into question the traditional theories concerning homosexuality. I have also critically examined the moral implications of certain methods of treatment, as well as some of the false transitions from psychological theory to moral judgment.

In their traditional presentation of moral obligation, Aquinas and Alphonsus Liguori, among others, always maintained *nulla obligatio imponatur nisi sit certa*. Given, as I believe, (1) the uncertainty of clear scriptural prohibition, (2) the questionable basis of the traditional condemnation in moral philosophy and moral theology, (3) the emergence of new data which upset many traditional assumptions, and (4) controversies among psychologists and psychiatrists concerning theory, etiology, treatment, and so on, there obviously is a need to open up anew the question of the moral standing of homosexual activity and homosexual relationships for public debate. Further, this debate must be public and cannot be limited to a peer-group discussion by experts, because the empirical experience of the Catholic homosexual community is a most important and even essential contribution for a successful outcome of that debate.

To anticipate for a moment the conclusion we will draw at the end of this work, it would appear to follow that the same moral rules apply to homosexual as to heterosexual attitudes and behavior. Those that are responsible, respectful, loving, and truly promotive of the good of both parties are moral; those that are exploitive, irresponsible, disrespectful, or destructive of the true good of either party must be judged immoral. I am aware that this conclusion moves beyond the position reached by many of my fellow theologians and the present teaching of the official magisterium. Some moralists, for example, insist that the connection between human sexuality and procreation is clearly established in Scripture. To quote one expert:

> In succinct form the biblical norm for human sexuality is this: man and woman joined together in one flesh in faithful love . . . specifically, the bind I feel is not located in the Christian norm itself. Theologically I subscribe to that norm with conviction. For me the problem lies in how the norm is used in Church and society; what is done by design or default to those who violate it. The homosexual bears pressures, indignities and injustices which demand relief. The question is how to take up his cause without either sacrificing the norm or sanctioning its use as a cover for persecution.

In the ongoing dialogue with this man and other moral theologians, the primary and most fundamental criticism I have received is that in attempting to discover a genuinely helpful pastoral approach I have come close to losing hold on that so-called biblical norm. Consequently, they claim that the burden of proof is on me to show that the man-woman relationship as traditionally understood in our culture is not "biblically and anthropologically normative." The entire first section of this book attempts to respond to that objection. I leave to the reader to decide whether or not I have adequately responded.

Another objection to my position arises from the belief of many moralists that the procreative framework provides the only valid ground for rational moral judgment and the only real corrective in society to hedonistic selfishness. Thus it is held that any moral approval of homosexual activity could result in a fundamental moral breakdown affecting the whole human community. As one critic suggests, my treatment of homosexuality implicitly opens up, but does not attempt to resolve, a host of other questions concerning sexual morality— such as premarital sex and extramarital sex—by challenging the marriage-and-procreation framework within which these questions have traditionally been resolved. In response to this objection I believe it is important, first of all, to grasp realistically the fact that owing to many factors—longer life-span, overpopulation, birth control, the women's liberation movement, the development of asexual means of procreation, and so on—the procreative context is necessarily breaking down and factually will no longer serve in the future as a practical means of regulating and judging the moral worth of the greater part of human sexual activity. Further, I believe that the interpersonal context properly understood (which is also a biblically approved, normative context) can and will provide an adequate framework for moral judgment and healthy regulation of human sexual activity both in heterosexual and in homosexual relationships. In this respect the emergence of a visible homosexual community both in society and in the Church can be seen as providential, because the homosexual community must perforce learn to deal with human sexuality outside the context of procreation. Their own happiness and human fulfillment demand that they find in the framework of interpersonal relationships those forms of sexual expression which can be healthy and conducive to growth. In searching out this framework, the homosexual community could supply the entire human community with irreplaceable empirical evidence on how sexual morality and sexual mores must change in the future.

There is still another set of criticisms to which I would like to respond briefly. Some readers of my manuscript have thought that my treatment of this subject is too partisan. They see me as a proponent of "advocacy theology," giving a strong bias to one side of the question. These readers seem to miss the point that almost everything that has been written in the past in moral theology concerning homosexuality has been "advocacy theology" biased in a negative direction. I leave to the reader the judgment of whether or not my treatment is biased. For my part, I did my best to present fairly all the evidence for and against each thesis I dealt with. I never deliberately omitted or distorted any evidence, even though it was contrary to my convictions. However, even if there is an element of truth in this criticism, I would still feel justified in my approach. For too long all we have seen is writing and counseling biased in the other direction. One of my goals is to open up a new dialogue by pushing the dialogical pendulum a bit in the opposite direction.

This reappraisal opens up the possibility of a new dimension to the theological evaluation of homosexuality. If homosexuality is not necessarily contrary to nature and the divine will, then the question may be posed: For what purpose does the homosexual exist? What positive contribution can the homosexual make to the human community as such? The second part of this study explores this teleological aspect of homosexuality. It is my deepest conviction that only by trying to respond to these questions can the moral theologian deal adequately with the human phenomenon of homosexuality; only thus can a positive understanding of that phenomenon be achieved, an understanding which can effectively destroy the grounds of prejudice, injustice, and persecution and liberate the homosexual to make his positive contribution to the development of a more human community.

After summarizing the various grounds for a reevaluation of homosexuality from the viewpoint of moral theology in Part 1 of this study, and exploring the positive contribution that the homosexual community can make to human development in Part 2, we attempt in Part 3 to explore in outline the implications for pastoral practice in terms of both individual counseling and institutional policy. The Christians who without any fault of their own share the homosexual condition are a very real factor in our midst. Perhaps no single group of human beings has been subjected to greater injustice, persecution, and suffering than they. And, even if inculpably, the Church shares a heavy burden of responsibility for this situation. The single purpose which has inspired this study has been to make some effort to understand the problem of the believing homosexuals and to offer practical and responsible solutions to the dilemma they face, solutions compatible with our present state of knowledge and with the deepest implications of Christian faith and morality.

I am particularly indebted to Charles Curran for providing the inspiration especially for the first part of this study. His book *Catholic Moral Theology in Dialogue* contains a chapter, entitled "Dialogue with the Homophile Movement: The

Morality of Homosexuality," in which he outlines the methodological and substantive considerations which must enter into moral theology's evaluation of homosexuality. While agreeing for the most part with his methodology, I have found it necessary on several occasions to respectfully disagree with his conclusions. A critical reflection on Curran's chapter convinced me that I should attempt to put into writing the experience and the various criticisms which have occurred to me over the past five years, since the publication of my article "The Christian Homosexual" in the *Homiletic and Pastoral Review*.

Part 1

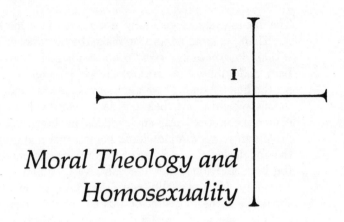

I

Moral Theology and Homosexuality

The Present Situation

The chapter entitled "Dialogue with the Homophile Movement: The Morality of Homosexuality" in Father Curran's recent book *Catholic Moral Theology in Dialogue*[1] represents an important contribution, made by an outstanding professional moral theologian in the Catholic Church, to a serious reconsideration of the Church's attitude toward the homosexual. Father Curran's position merits serious consideration by the Catholic homophile community in order to discern both the advanced understanding of their situation that it manifests and the limits of that understanding, and especially the value of the reasoning Father Curran advances in defense of those limits.

Although he finds himself in disagreement with the reasoning I employed in my earlier article, "The Christian Male Homosexual" in the *Homiletic and Pastoral Review*,[2] as he understands it, Curran says he finds himself "in general agreement with the practical conclusions proposed by McNeill." In his own words, he summarizes these conclusions as follows:

29

The homosexual is generally not responsible for his condition. . . . Therapy, as an attempt to make the homosexual into a heterosexual, does not offer great promise for most homosexuals. Celibacy and sublimation are not always possible or even desirable for the homosexual. There are many somewhat stable homosexual unions which afford their partners some human fulfillment and contentment. Obviously such unions are better than homosexual promiscuity . . . the individual homosexual may morally come to the conclusion that a somewhat permanent homosexual union is the best, and sometimes the only, way for him to achieve some humanity. Homosexuality can never become an ideal. Attempts should be made to overcome this condition if possible; however, at times one may reluctantly accept homosexual unions as the only way in which some people can find a satisfying degree of humanity in their lives.[3]

I will discuss further the respects in which my own conclusions differ from those of Curran. But the point I would like to make at the beginning is that these practical conclusions which Curran accepts represent a substantial advance over the traditional position in Catholic moral theology, which tended in the past to see all homosexual relations as subjectively and objectively mortally sinful and thus left the Catholic homosexual no morally acceptable alternative except a life of total abstinence from sexual activity. In practice these conclusions imply that under certain conditions a Catholic homosexual can enter into an active homosexual relationship and still receive the sacraments and live a life of sexual love which does not necessarily separate him or her from the love of God in Christ.

What are the limits, however, which Curran finds necessary to place on the Church's moral acceptance of homosexuality? He speaks of his theory as a "theory of compromise":

In the theory of compromise, the particular action [homosexual] in one sense is not objectively wrong because in the presence of sin it remains the only viable alternative for the individual. How-

ever, in another sense the action is wrong and manifests the
power of sin. If possible, man must try to overcome sin, but the
Christian knows that the struggle against sin is never totally successful in this world.[4]

These limitations carry with them the logical implication that
while Catholic homosexuals may be morally justified in entering into a homosexual relationship temporarily, owing to their
objectively sinful condition, they must continue to do everything in their power to free themselves from their need of
that relationship, since it represents the power of sin over
them.

At the beginning of his article Curran acknowledges that a
moral study should not be done independent of its relation to
pastoral practice. "This study should, however, furnish a basis
for forming a proper pastoral approach to the homosexual and
the homophile community. . . ."[5] At the end of the article
he reverts to the pastoral implications of his moral theory by
conceding: "One can object that such a view still relegates
the homosexual to second-class citizenship."[6] But, he responds,
"one can still love and respect the person even though one
believes his homosexual behavior falls short of the full meaning of human sexuality. In many other areas of life I can judge
a person's behavior as being wrong or less than ideal and still
respect him as a person."[7] Curran probably has in mind here
the objection on the part of Catholic homosexuals against the
tendency of many priests to pass objective moralistic judgments
that render their pastoral counseling ineffective. I believe he
misses the point of the objection. The problem is not the
ability of the confessor or counselor to pass judgment on the
homosexual condition as an objective manifestation of sin,
whatever may be the truth of that judgment, while still
respecting the individual as person. The problem, rather, is
the homosexual's consequent judgment on himself, or herself,

if the judgment that the homosexual condition is objectively sinful is uncritically accepted by the person in question.[8]

How can Christian homosexuals accept themselves and their homosexuality with any sense of their own dignity and value as long as they must see themselves and their actions as organically expressing the effects of sin in the world and as essentially in contradiction to the divine will for man? How can individuals with such an understanding of themselves possibly enter into a constructive homosexual relationship which expresses true human love? Curran's position calls to mind an article by Joseph Epstein in *Harper's Magazine*.[9] While professing many liberal attitudes toward the homosexual, Epstein concludes his article by comparing him to the leper of Old Testament times. Epstein's culturally conditioned emotional revulsion is so strong that he even avows he would rather see his own sons dope addicts or murderers than to see them become homosexuals. One cannot help thinking what would be the suffering of one of Epstein's sons if he should, God forbid, find himself a homosexual. In an analogous way the homosexual who accepts Curran's judgment must see himself condemned through no fault of his own to a life in which every expression of human sexual love will only serve to deepen the hold of an objectively sinful condition on himself and his loved one, separating them further from God's plan. In contradiction to the biblical message that it is by love that one unites oneself to God, the homosexual must see his deepest and most sincere human love as cutting him and his loved one off from God.

Curran seems to accept the questionable theological position that every affliction is the result of sin and that the sins of parents are punished in their offspring. For he states at one point that homosexuality is "a result of sin," and appears to accept the unproven causal assumption that the homosexuality of the child is a result of sinful failures in parental relationships: "Those who accept an etiology of homosexuality in terms of relationships and environment can easily see the reality of sin in the poor relationships and environment which contribute to this condition in the individual."[10] Needless to say, this understanding of the source of homosexuality has been seriously discredited by many professional studies. As Dennis Altman notes:

> Many psychiatrists tend to locate the origins of homosexuality in "maladjusted" family life, yet such an explanation is not altogether convincing. Too many homosexuals have strong and loving fathers, too many heterosexuals have dominating mothers, for any very obvious connection to be seen. It is probable that in Western societies most mothers overdominate their sons, and this fact is often disregarded by those concerned to discover the etiology of homosexuality.[11]

Psychologist Ray B. Arens also points out that some consideration must be given to the likelihood that the child's inner character at least partially determines parental reactions and attitudes toward him: "For instance, it is just as tenable to assume that the father of a pre-homosexual son becomes detached or hostile because he does not understand his son, is disappointed in him, or threatened by him, as it is to assume that the son becomes homosexual because of the father's reaction."[12]

What is particularly reprehensible about this dubious assumption of parental fault is the unproven burden of guilt it imposes on parents and the added impediment it places in the way of their children's being able to share their problem with their family. There are no necessary grounds for judging parents somehow responsible for their son's or daughter's homosexual condition; but there may well be grounds for judging them responsible for the disturbed or neurotic condition that all too frequently accompanies homosexuality. For the real moral problem that exists for the parents of a homosexual child is one of loving openness and acceptance. Whenever, in counseling, one has the good fortune to encounter psychologically healthy homosexuals, sure of their own dignity and their power to love and to be loved, one can be almost certain that their parents, whatever their disappointment over their children's condition, have responded to them with true acceptance and love. Parents of a homosexual have no reason to assume guilt for their child's condition; but parents of a psychologically healthy homosexual have good reason to believe that they have done their difficult task well.

Curran to all appearances never takes the human love which unites homosexual partners seriously. One is left with the impression that he reluctantly admits the possibility of homosexual liaisons in the same spirit as civil authorities who "reluctantly" license houses of prostitution, for his reason for condoning the existence of such liaisons is that they would be "better than homosexual promiscuity." In this respect it is interesting to note Curran's misinterpretation of my articles in the *Homiletic and Pastoral Review*.[13] At one point I conceded to those of my readers who could not understand or accept an ethic based in interpersonal love that they could, perhaps, accept homosexual relationships as morally valid from the traditional viewpoint of "the lesser of two evils." This was only one passing aspect of my argument for the possibility of "ethically responsible homosexual relationships," a passing attempt to conciliate those who could not free themselves from the need of a traditional peg on which to hang their moral judgments.[14] However, the entire thrust of my argument for morally acceptable homosexual relationships was that this form of sexual expression could be morally justified if it could be expressive of genuinely constructive human love.

It should come as no surprise, then, that all the qualities which morally justify a heterosexual human relationship— fidelity and permanence, for example—are systematically negated by Curran in the context of homosexual relationships. Instead of being able to form the intention of fidelity and permanence in their human love relationships to the best of their ability, homosexuals who accept Curran's judgment must see their relationships as being morally justifiable only as a temporary concession to their moral deformity. Thus they must continue to do everything in their power to correct their condition, or at least abstain from an active expression of it— and consequently bring any homosexual love relationship to an end. The most important question, however, still remains unanswered: What methodological and substantive considerations led Curran into all the ambiguities of his theory of compromise?

II

Scripture and Homosexuality

The Use of Scripture

There are two methodological questions in moral theology which are important for a discussion of the morality of homosexuality. The first of these has to do with the use and place of Scripture in moral theology, and the second with the use and place of the human sciences. Since a Christian ethics as such reflects on human reality within the context of Christian revelation, it is obvious that scriptural sources have a role to play: "Biblical ethics contributes data to Christian ethics, but it remains only one aspect, albeit a privileged aspect, of the total data of ethical theology," Father Curran notes. There are, however, two limitations to the use of biblical data. First, the Scriptures are "historically and culturally limited," so that one cannot merely transpose a text of Scripture to the contemporary circumstances of life. Secondly, no thesis would be acceptable which would develop its argument only in terms of individual texts taken out of their context.[15]

When Curran makes use of scriptural data concerning homosexuality, however, he does not seem to apply adequately the criteria he himself set down for a legitimate use of such data.

Referring to those passages in the Old and New Testaments which have been traditionally translated as dealing with homosexuality, he acknowledges that "possibly erroneous interpretations seem to have overemphasized the heinousness of homosexual acts."[16] He accepts D. Sherwin Bailey's account of the Sodom story of Genesis 19:4–11, granting that the sin of the Sodomites "does not necessarily involve a sexual connotation but could be interpreted as a violation of hospitality."[17] This is a very important concession, since the centuries-old tradition in the Christian world of extreme condemnation of homosexuality always had its primary basis in the interpretation of this text of Genesis as indicating an extreme divine judgment of condemnation on homosexual behavior. He continues to accept, however, what he believes to be a general condemnation of homosexuality in the Old Testament. His primary evidence for this is the references to homosexuality in the Holiness Code (Lev. 18:22; 20:13), where it is referred to as a major crime punishable by death.

Indicating three direct references to homosexuality in the New Testament, all in the epistles of St. Paul (1 Cor. 6:9–10; 1 Tim. 1:9–10; Rom. 1:26–27), Curran concludes: "Paul obviously regards homosexual acts as wrong and a perversion of human existence willed by God."[18] He acknowledges, however, Thielicke's contention that Paul's consideration of homosexuality appears "only in the context of a more central theological affirmation that disorder in the vertical dimension of man's relation with God is matched by disorder in the horizontal dimension."[19] Consequently, Paul never considers homosexuality in itself, but "only as illustrative of the central theological point that man's relationship with God affects all his other relationships."[20]

Curran concludes from this brief consideration of biblical data that it "indicates that the biblical authors in their cultural and historical circumstances deemed homosexual acts wrong

and attached a generic gravity to such acts, but there appears
to be no reason for attaching a special heinousness or gravity
to these acts."[21] In all these considerations, however, he omits
a central question. Can one merely accept what is referred to
in English translations of the Bible as homosexuality as repre-
senting in the mind of the biblical authors what we refer to
today by the same term?

We would do well to recall here the words of the Dogmatic
Constitution on Divine Revelation of the Second Vatican Council dealing with the interpretation of sacred Scripture:

> Since God speaks in sacred Scripture through men in a human
> fashion, the interpreter of sacred Scripture, in order to see
> clearly what God wanted to communicate to us, should carefully
> investigate what meaning the sacred writers really intended, and
> what God wanted to manifest by means of their words. (No.
> 12)[22]

This cautious investigation of the intention of the human
author is especially called for in dealing with biblical passages
which traditionally have been accepted as dealing with homosexual activity.

The Need for a Definition of Homosexuality

Unfortunately, Curran never attempts to define exactly what
he means by the term homosexual. As a result he feels free to
assume that what is usually translated in the biblical texts by
the same term as that used today actually refers to the same
condition. It can, however, be argued (1) that what is referred to, especially in the New Testament, under the rubric
of homosexuality is not the same reality at all or (2) that the
biblical authors do not manifest the same understanding of
that reality as we have today. Further, it can be seriously
questioned whether what is understood today as the true
homosexual and his or her activity is ever the object of explicit moral condemnation in Scripture.

The prefix "homo" in the word homosexual is derived from the Greek root meaning "same," and not from the Latin word for "man." Consequently, it designates anyone who is sexually attracted to someone of the same sex and includes both male and female homosexuals, or lesbians. Most human beings are capable of either homosexual or heterosexual activity, independent of the question of their own psychological sexual orientation. Many homosexuals marry and have children, frequently in an effort to conceal their sexual orientation. On the other hand, there is no necessary connection between overt homosexual behavior and the permanent psychological condition of homosexuality. Many people have had homosexual experiences who do not have a predominantly homosexual orientation but are definitely heterosexually inclined. Consequently, it is important for the moralist to keep the distinction between homosexual activity and the homosexual condition clearly in mind. For there is an important difference in the moral judgment to be passed on a heterosexual indulging in homosexual activity and a true homosexual indulging in the same behavior as an expression of his or her love.

Kinsey limited himself exclusively to objective behavior in the scientific study he made of sexual mores in the United States, leaving aside the subjective question of the sexual orientation of his respondents. According to Kinsey, as much as thirty-seven percent of the male population had some overt homosexual experience.[23] In the majority of cases, however, these experiences seemed to involve little more than transitory experimentation which did not inhibit a later satisfactory heterosexual adjustment. There are many other forms of contingent homosexual practice which can be called situational and which do not indicate a true homosexual psychological condition. When, for example, men are isolated together for long periods of time and separated from the companionship of women—as in prisons or at sea—many will adopt homosexual behavior; but most of them normally discard their homosexual behavior and resume a heterosexual orientation once withdrawn from their segregated situation. Still other forms of conditional homosexual behavior, which do not necessarily indicate a homosexual condition, can be called variational, e.g. heterosexuals who occasionally take part in homosexual activity out of curiosity or as an easy means of sexual indulgence. Still one other form of conditional homosexual behavior should be mentioned; this category involves people who, although they are fundamentally heterosexually inclined, adopt homosexual behavior consequent upon some traumatic event or psychic disorder. If they are cured of their trauma or disorder, they will revert to their original heterosexual inclination.

Although all of the above groups have had some homosexual experience, none of them are what could be called "true" homosexuals. Today we use the word homosexual primarily to refer to the psychic condition of the individual, and not just to occasional behavior. Bailey defines homosexuality as "a condition characterized by an emotional and physicosexual propensity toward others of the same sex."[24] D. W. Cory defines the homosexual as "any person who feels a most urgent sexual desire which in the main is directed toward gratification with the same sex."[25] The Dutch Cathechism uses the term to refer to those "whose eroticism cannot be directed to the other sex, but apparently only to the same sex to which they themselves belong."[26] As John Cavanaugh remarks, "It is important to accept the concept that homosexuality is a way of thinking and feeling, not merely a way of acting. The performance of homosexual acts is, therefore, not in itself evidence of homosexuality."[27] Christopher Isherwood indicates the subjective norm for knowing oneself to be a homosexual when he writes: "You first *know* you are a homosexual when you fall in love with another man."[28]

As Bailey observes, strictly speaking neither the Bible nor Christian tradition knew anything of homosexuality as such; both were concerned solely with the commission of homosexual acts.[29] Homosexuality is not, as commonly supposed, a kind of conduct, but a psychological condition. It is important to understand that the genuine homosexual condition—or inversion, as it is often termed—is something for which the subject can in no way be held responsible. In itself it is morally neutral. Like the condition of heterosexuality, however, it tends to find expression in specific sexual acts; and such acts are subject to moral judgment. We must distinguish, then, between the invert and the pervert. The pervert is not a genuine homosexual; rather, he is a heterosexual who engages in homosexual practices, or a homosexual who engages in heterosexual practices. This distinction between the condition of inversion and the behavior of perversion is indispensable for a correct interpretation of biblical and traditional sources.

The real moral problem of homosexuality has to do with judging the moral value of sexual activity between genuine homosexuals who seek to express their love for one another in a sexual gesture. Scripture can be understood as clearly and explicitly condemning true homosexual activity only if it can be interpreted as condemning the activity of a true invert. To such situations, however, it can hardly be said that the Bible addresses itself, since the condition of inversion with all its special problems was quite unknown at the time. On the contrary, there is ample evidence that in most instances where Scripture deals with homosexuality the author probably had in mind what today we would call perversion, namely, the indulgence in homosexual activity on the part of those who were by nature heterosexually inclined.

The Sodom and Gomorrah Story in Genesis

Perhaps the single most important factor in the Western

Christian tradition condemning homosexual practices is the interpretation given to the Sodom and Gomorrah story in Genesis 19:4–11.[30] The Church taught, and people universally believed on what they held to be excellent authority, that homosexual practices had brought a terrible divine vengeance upon the cities of Sodom and Gomorrah, and that the repetition of such "offences against nature" had from time to time provoked similar visitations of divine wrath in the form of earthquakes, floods, famines, outbreaks of pestilence, etc. It was taken for granted, therefore, that by means of both Church discipline and the restraints and penalties of civil law steps should be taken to ward off the wrath of God from the community. It was also taken for granted that the sin for which the cities of the plain were destroyed was that of the habitual indulgence of perverse homosexual practices among men. Consequently, the question must be posed: To what extent is this tradition truly founded in Scripture? What was the meaning of the encounter of Lot and his angelic visitors with the angry inhabitants of Sodom as recorded by the Yahwist author of Genesis 19? Finally, what grounds, if any, are there for the persistent belief that the inhabitants of the city were addicted to male homosexual practices and were punished accordingly?

As D. S. Bailey points out, the attribution of homosexual practices is based usually on the demand the Sodomites are recorded to have made of Lot: "Bring them [Lot's visitors] out unto us, that we may know them." The Hebrew word "to know" (yādhá) can mean "engage in coitus." However, Bailey argues this is not necessarily the meaning of the word in this passage. The Hebrew-English Lexicon of the Old Testament notes that of the 943 uses of yādhá, it is used only 10 times without qualification, apart from this text in Genesis and its derivative in Judges 19:22, to denote sexual coitus. And, again with the possible exception of this text, it always refers to heterosexual coitus. The word normally used in the Old Testament for both homosexual coitus and bestiality is *shākhabh*. G. A. Barton concludes from this evidence that "there is no actual necessity to interpret 'know' in Gen. xix, 5 as equivalent with 'to have coitus with.' It may mean no more than 'get acquainted with.' "[31]

Bailey argues further that the passage can be interpreted as implying that Lot, who was a *gēr* or resident alien in Sodom, may have exceeded his rights by receiving and entertaining two foreigners whose intentions might have been hostile and whose credentials, it seems, had not been examined. This explanation provides a natural and sufficient reason for the demand: "Where are the men who came to thee this night? Bring them out unto us, that we may know them."

What, then, Bailey asks, was the nature of the sinfulness of Sodom and Gomorrah? We are told in the passage itself in Genesis that these cities were wicked and grievously sinful, but the writer does not specify the nature of this iniquity more exactly. However, Bailey argues, only on a priori grounds can it be assumed that it was an iniquity solely or even predominantly sexual in character. There is no evidence elsewhere in the passage or in the Old Testament to show that homosexual behavior was particularly prevalent in these cities. Lot's offer to surrender his daughters in place of the strangers is sometimes interpreted as an offer of heterosexual in lieu of homosexual satisfaction, in order to divert the lust of the Sodomites into less inordinate channels. However, Bailey claims, this episode can be reasonably explained as simply the most tempting bribe Lot could offer at the spur of the moment to appease a hostile crowd.

Bailey believes that for an understanding of the development of the Sodom and Gomorrah story it is important to place it in the context of the legends of a similar character in the folk-

lore of the surrounding cultures. Many of these legends tell of
a stranger (sometimes a divine being in disguise) who visits a
prosperous city and is refused hospitality. He eventually finds
a lodging, often with poor outcasts. Consequently, he helps
his hosts escape before the city and its inhabitants are destroyed. The most famous of these legends is Ovid's account
of Philemon and Baucis.[32] These legends may account for the
particular form the Sodom story itself assumed during its
course of oral transmission prior to being written down. In
the legend, as in the same Yahwist author's Tower of Babel
narrative in Genesis 11:9, the conduct which brings judgment
upon the offending community and leads to its destruction is
never sexual, but always wickedness in general, and in particular pride and inhospitality.

There are several other aspects to the narrative, besides
those Bailey mentions, which tend to indicate that in the mind
of the Yahwist author of the narrative the sin of Sodom and
Gomorrah was primarily one of inhospitality to strangers. For
example, when the angelic visitors come as strangers to
Abraham's tent, the quality of Abraham as a good man is
dramatically established by an emphasis on his hospitable
reception of the strangers.

> Raising his eyes he saw three men standing near him. On seeing
> them, he ran from the door of his tent to meet them, and bow-
> ing to the ground said; "Oh sirs, if perchance I find favor with
> you, please do not pass by without stopping with your servant.
> Let a little water be brought to wash your feet, and stretch your-
> selves out under the tree, while I fetch a bit of food that you may
> refresh yourselves. Afterwards you may proceed on your way,
> since you will then have paid your servant a visit." (Gen. 18:1-
> 5)[33]

Similarly the quality of Lot as a good man worthy of God's
favor is established in contrast to the other inhabitants of
Sodom by his hospitality to the same strangers in terms

strongly reminiscent of the story of the disciples of Emmaus in the New Testament:

> The two angels arrived at Sodom in the evening while Lot was sitting at the gate of Sodom. When Lot saw them, he rose to greet them, bowing his face to the ground, and saying: "If you please, sirs, come over to your servant's house to pass the night and wash your feet; in the morning you may rise early, and go on your way." But they said: "No, we will pass the night in the open." He pressed them so strongly, however, that they went over to his house, where he prepared a feast for them, and baked unleavened bread for them to eat. (Gen. 19:1–3)

A confirmation of the interpretation of the primary sin of Sodom and Gomorrah as inhospitality occurs in the New Testament where Christ is recorded as discussing the problem of the inhospitable reception of his disciples:

> But whenever you come to a town and they do not welcome you, go out into the open streets and say: "The very dust of your town that sticks to our feet we wipe off in protest. But understand this: The Kingdom of God is at hand!" I tell you, on that day Sodom will fare better than that town! (Lk. 10:10–13)

Throughout the Old Testament Sodom is referred to as a symbol of utter destruction occasioned by sins of such magnitude as to merit exemplary punishment.[34] However, nowhere in the Old Testament is that sin identified explicitly with homosexual behavior. In Ezekiel 16:49–50, for example, we read: "Behold, this was the sin of your sister Sodom: she and her daughters lived in pride, plenty, and thoughtless ease; they supported not the poor and needy; they grew haughty, and committed abomination before me; so I swept them away, as you have seen." Isaiah stresses lack of justice, Jeremiah cites moral and ethical laxity. The Deuterocanonical books usually identify the sin as one of pride and inhospitality. Wisdom (19:13–14), for example, clearly identifies the sin as one of inhospitality: ". . . whereas the men of Sodom received not the strangers when they came among them; the Egyptians made slaves of the guests who were their bene-factors." Ecclesiasticus (16:8) in turn identifies the sin as pride: "He did not spare the people among whom Lot was living, whom he detested for their pride." Only the late New Testament books, 2 Peter and Jude, find the sin of Sodom connected in any way with sexual practices; but these books, as we shall discuss later, seem to understand the sin as a "transgression of orders" between human and angelic beings.

A further confirmation that in biblical times the sin of Sodom was not connected with homosexual practices as such is to be found in the fact that none of the biblical passages, either in the Old or New Testament, traditionally understood as condemning these practices makes any mention of the Sodom story. Yet such a reference would have been obvious if the sin of Sodom was understood as involving these practices.

It would seem fairly certain, then, that the sin of Sodom was understood in biblical times as primarily one of inhos-pitality. However, Bailey may perhaps have overstated his case in maintaining that there is no reference at all to sexual mistreatment of the strangers as one aspect of the crime of inhospitality. There is a hint of this in the fact that the same Hebrew word *yādhá* is used again by Lot in verse 7 when he offers his daughters to the inhabitants, and here it clearly and unambiguously implies sexual knowledge:

> Please my friends, be not so depraved. I have two daughters who have never had intercourse (yādhá) with a man, let me bring them out to you that you may do with them what you will; only do nothing to these men, inasmuch as they have come under the shelter of my roof. (Gen. 19:7–8)

It remains possible, however, that the Yahwist author was deliberately playing on the ambiguity of the term, using it in two different meanings.

Further, Bailey's interpretation makes it difficult to understand how the behavior of the inhabitants of Sodom confirmed the angels' opinion that they were wicked enough to deserve divine punishment, if they only wished to examine their credentials. In the derivative account of the crime of Gibeah in the Book of Judges (19:1–21:25), the identical request is made of the old man, who takes in the stranger for the night, by the inhabitants of Gibeah. In this instance, however, the stranger releases his female consort to the crowd, and they so misuse her sexually that the stranger finds her dead on the threshold in the morning. At a consequent gathering of the tribes of Israel, the stranger makes clear what the crime of Gibeah was:

> To Gibeah, which belongs to the Benjamin, I came with my consort to spend the night; but the citizens of Gibeah rose against me, and at night surrounded the house against me. Me they intended to kill, and my consort they ravished, so that she died. (Judg. 20:4–6)

In the book of Judges' derivative, then, the crime of inhospitality included the design to murder the stranger. The obvious stress, once again, is not so much on the implied sexual contact with the stranger as on the right of the stranger to a hospitable reception. John McKenzie's comment on the crime of Gibeah is equally applicable to the Sodom story:

> They [the authors] here betray two convictions . . . the absolute sacredness of the guest and the absolute dignity of the male sex. The duty of the host to protect the guest we can understand, but not to the point where the honor and the life of the women of the family are regarded as expendable.[35]

As we shall note later, the idea of "the absolute dignity of the male sex" was one of the factors underlying the Jewish hostility to male homosexual practices.

Peter Ellis, in his book *The Yahwist: The Bible's First*

Theologian, offers an interesting and suggestive thesis to explain the possible presence of the sexual element in the Sodom narrative. He points out that one of the Yahwist author's principal themes was an attack against Canaanite nature worship directed to the fertility Gods. Speaking of the episode in Genesis concerning the "sons of God" lusting after the daughters of men, he writes:

> The Yahwist's audience would certainly recognize in the story an allusion to the ludicrous belief of the Canaanite religion that by means of sacred prostitution—sexual intercourse with male and female prostitutes at the Canaanite shrines—it was possible to enter into special relationship with the god or goddess represented by the sacred prostitute.[36]

In the fertility-cult ritual, sacred prostitution climaxed the rite which hailed the return of the rains and fertility. "In the punishment which follows the fornication of the sons of God with the daughters of men the rains came with a vengeance. The floods cover the earth, and everything upon its fertile surface is swept away by cleansing waters."[37]

Ellis suggests that the same polemic against the fertility rites is to be found in the Sodom narrative. "For their crimes, which the author indicates were the unnatural sexual vices the Canaanites had made part of their fertility rites, the five plain cities are wiped off the map."[38] The same connection between homosexual practices and idolatry which, as we shall see, is present in all the biblical passages is also present here. Again, the punishment is a "rain"; this time a rain of fire and brimstone, and the result is a barren earth on which nothing will ever grow. Even in this interpretation, the primary crime of Sodom is idolatry, and not homosexual practices as such but these practices as an expression of sacred prostitution.

We shall deal later, under the heading of tradition, with the gradual historical development which transformed the understanding of the sin of Sodom in Western Christian tradition from a sin primarily of inhospitality to the stranger to one of homosexual practices. At this point we can conclude, however, that the most important biblical basis for the traditional condemnation of homosexual practices as clearly against the express will of God proves on examination the most vulnerable. It has been accepted practically without question that God himself declared his judgment upon homosexual practices once and for all time by the destruction of the cities of the plains. But the Sodom and Gomorrah narrative possibly had nothing whatever to do with such practices. Even if one continues to hold that there is a suggestion of the presence of this sexual element, it does not constitute the essence of the sin of Sodom and Gomorrah. Rather, the sin remains primarily one of inhospitality. And even if Ellis is correct, the homosexual practices are condemned not in themselves but as part of the idolatrous fertility cult of the Canaanites.

If this interpretation of the true sin of Sodom is correct, then we are dealing here with one of the supremely ironic paradoxes of history. For thousands of years in the Christian West the homosexual has been the victim of inhospitable treatment. Condemned by the Church, he has been the victim of persecution, torture, and even death. In the name of a mistaken understanding of the crime of Sodom and Gomorrah, the true crime of Sodom and Gomorrah has been and continues to be repeated every day. Before advancing to an examination of the Sodom story in tradition, let us first examine the other passages in the Old and New Testaments understood as condemning homosexual practices.

Problems of Translation

Two Greek words in 1 Cor. 6:9 are usually translated as having to do with homosexuality; they are *malakói* and *ársenokóitai*. The second term occurs again in 1 Tim. 1:10.

There is a venerable tradition in English translations of the Bible to assume that these terms apply to homosexual activity. The King James version translates them as "neither the effeminate nor the abusers of themselves with mankind" and the Rheims-Douai version similarly speaks of the "effeminate" and "liers with mankind." The first edition of the Revised Standard version translates both terms with the one word "homosexuals." The only major variation of this tradition is to be found in the Jerusalem Bible, which uses the terms "catamites and sodomites," and the Smith-Goodspeed (Chicago) Bible, which renders them as "sensual" and those "given to unnatural vices." It is interesting to note that the Spanish version of the Jerusalem Bible uses "los homosexuales," whereas the French version speaks of "depraves" and "gens de moeurs infames." As John Boswell notes: "Cultural differences appear to exercise considerable influence over the translation of Biblical passages dealing with sexual morality."[39] Bailey particularly takes to task the translators of the Revised Standard version for their use of the single term "homosexuals":

> But the translation approved by those responsible for the American Revised Standard version is unfortunately both inaccurate and objectionable . . . it is most regrettable that the reviewers should have shown themselves unaware or unappreciative of the clear distinction which must be made between the homosexual *condition* (which is morally neutral) and homosexual *practices*. Use of the word "homosexuals" inevitably suggests the genuine invert, even though he be a man of irreproachable morals, is automatically branded as unrighteous and excluded from the kingdom of God, just as if he were the most depraved of sexual perverts.[40]

The variation in translations points to the fact that there is very little understanding of the precise meaning of Paul's terms. What is needed is a contextual analysis and an examination of the same terms in other sources. It is truly surprising that despite the fact that the tradition of moral condemnation of homosexuality springs in large part from these biblical passages, little serious scholarly work has been produced concerning their exact meaning. Translations appear at times to be based on preconceptions rather than serious scholarship.

The immediate context itself gives little or no clue as to the precise meaning Paul intended by these words. In the Corinthian passage Paul lists the types of sinners who are to be excluded from the kingdom of God; and in the Timothy passage, those who have not received the law of God.

S. Wibbing argues that Paul derived these lists from the popular Stoic list of excesses contrary to reason.[41] Both lists have been recognized by scholars as remarkably confusing, and the context is quite loose. Consequently we must turn to the use of the same terms in other sources to discover their meaning. The word *malakós* literally means soft (e.g., Luke 7:25; Mt. 11:8). In a moral context it is normally employed to signify loose, morally weak, or lacking in self-control. There is no justification for applying *malakós* specifically to homosexuality. In patristic Greek *malakía* usually referred to generally dissolute behavior and occasionally referred to specific sexual activity such as masturbation, but never to homosexuality as such. It could conceivably include that, but its normal use referred to any form of immorality. I need not stress the point here that the concept of "effeminacy" has no necessary connection with homosexuality.[42]

Before considering the second word, *ársenokóitai*, it is important to recall to mind that there was no word in classical, biblical, or patristic Greek with the same meaning as the English word homosexual. In those pre-Freudian days neither the Greeks nor the Romans recognized homosexuality as a psychological phenomenon or condition apart from general sexual behavior. There appears to be no consciousness of a dichotomy such as the modern homosexual versus heterosexual. There were names, however, for persons who practiced homosexual activity. They included, for example, *paiderastês, pallakós, kínaidos, árrenomanês,* and *paidophthóros.* If it were Paul's intention to indicate general homosexual activity as such, it is probable that he would have selected one of these terms.

The word *ársenokóitai,* then, probably does not refer to general homosexual behavior. However, what Paul did mean by it is difficult to ascertain. The use of the noun in the plural does not occur in Greek literature before the Pauline text. Apart from a second-century use of the same word in the *Apology* of Aristides, where from the context it seems to mean "an obsessive corruptor of boys,"[43] the most important usage for the purpose of clearer definition occurs in the sixth-century *Penitentiale* of Joannes Jejunator, Patriarch of Constantinople in 586 under Mauritius.[44] Here it designates a specific sex act, most likely anal intercourse. Nor does this refer exclusively to homosexuality, since in a later passage use is made of the same term to refer to a sex act between men and women.[45]

Some indication of what Paul might have meant by the term can be derived from his use of *kóitai* in the plural. For this usage appears to refer to excess in sexual behavior (cf. Rom. 13:13). It is possible that the author attached to the compound a meaning like "male prostitution." This interpretation is borne out by the Vulgate rendering *masculi concubitores,* that is, male concubines. As we shall see, this interpretation will be strengthened by the more general context of the Old Testament where male prostitution was usually associated with the same context of idolatry.

The Interpretation of Romans 1:26

The strongest New Testament argument against homosexual activity as intrinsically immoral has been derived traditionally from Romans 1:26, where this activity is indicted as *parà phúsin*. The normal English translation for this phrase has been "against nature." As John Boswell notes: "The modern reader is apt to read into that phrase a wealth of associations derived from later philosophical developments, scholastic theology, Freudian psychology, social taboos, as well as personal misgivings."[46] Once again it is difficult to ascertain what this phrase meant for Paul. The same phrase in Romans 4:18 is used to express the idea that God himself is acting *parà phúsin* in grafting a wild olive branch (the Gentiles) onto a cultivated tree (the inheritance of the Jews). This usage makes it clear that the phrase itself does not necessarily imply a moral judgment on the action as wrong.

From an examination of the seven uses of the word *phúsis* in the epistles of Paul, one can begin to understand what Paul meant by the word. Although it is most likely that Paul accepted the phrase from the popular Stoic philosophy of the day, he does not necessarily indicate an intrinsic nature or essence in the philosophical sense, such as would serve the basis of a natural-law judgment. Rather, it is always linked to religious and cultural heritage. The Jews are Jews "by nature" (Gal. 2:15); and the Gentiles are uncircumcised "by nature" (Rom. 2:27). Although we are all "by nature" children of wrath (Eph. 2:3), the Gentiles can do "by nature"—i.e. by custom without hearing the word—the things of the law (Rom. 2:14). With the exception of Gal. 4:8, where reference is made to men who "by nature" are not gods, the character referred to by *phúsis* does not necessarily represent something that is innate, but could be a matter of training and social conditioning. This is evident, for example, in 1 Cor. 11:14: "Does not nature teach you that, if a man has long hair, it is a shame unto him?"

When he uses the word nature Paul does not make a sharp distinction between natural law and social custom. For example, in the phrase *tēn phusikēn krēsin* (Rom. 1:26) Paul does not make the distinction between nature and custom which was common among educated Greeks of the time (e.g., *Ignatius to the Trallians* 1.1: "either against custom [*krēsin*] or nature [*phúsin*]"). Rather, he tends to fuse together the concepts of custom and essential character. There seems to be a parallel in Paul's mind between what is *parà phúsin* and the Old Testament concept of *toevah*, i.e. what is not proper according to Jewish law and custom.

Consequently, two interpretations can be justified concerning what Paul meant by the phrase. It could refer to the individual pagan, who goes beyond his own sexual appetites in order to indulge in new sexual pleasures. A strong argument for this interpretation is the explicit reference to the pagans having "abandoned" the "natural uses" of their sexuality for that which is "beyond nature." The use here of the aorist participle (*aphéntes*) considerably strengthens the image of a conscious choice of a type of activity contrary to their normal inclinations. Paul apparently refers only to homosexual acts indulged in by those he considered to be otherwise heterosexually inclined; acts which represent a voluntary choice to act contrary to their ordinary sexual appetite. William G. Thompson, S.J., is inclined to agree with this interpretation:

> Concerning the Pauline material, you have come to the same conclusions I have concerning the meaning of "homosexual." Let me quote Fr. Fitzmyer's comments on Romans 1:26: "The contrast between 'females' and 'males' (1:27) makes it clear that the sexual perversion of which Paul speaks is homosexuality (specifically Lesbianism). The depravity of the perversion is the merited consequence of pagan impiety; having exchanged their true God for a false one (1:25), pagans inevitably exchanged their true natural functions for perverted ones . . . (Jerome Biblical Commentary, Article 53, Number 26)." It seems clear that the situation is one of perversion rather than inversion, as you indicate. Hence the passage does not touch the contem-

porary issue of homosexuality understood as inversion. Paul simply does not speak to that question.

The second possibility is that *phúsis* refers to the "nature" of the chosen people who were forbidden by Levitical law to have homosexual relations. Paul can be understood as arguing that the recognition of the true God necessarily involves acceptance of the Levitical law. Both interpretations are probably valid. Paul seems to be implying that the Gentiles, having known the truth of God and rejecting it, as a result reject their true nature as regards their sexual appetites, going beyond what was natural to them (heterosexual activity) and what was approved for the Jews.

Consequently, the Pauline epistles do not explicitly treat of the problem of homosexual activity between persons who share the homosexual condition, and as such cannot be read as explicitly condemning such behavior. Neither the *malakói* nor the *arsenokóitai* were necessarily homosexuals; the former were simply debauched individuals and the latter were probably male prostitutes or those given to anal intercourse, which is not necessarily nor exclusively an homosexual activity. The persons referred to in Romans 1:26 are probably not homosexuals—i.e. those who are psychologically inclined toward their own sex—since they are portrayed as "abandoning their natural customs." Moreover, the ambiguity of Paul's use of the word *phúsis* as including what is customary precludes an interpretation of the passage as condemning homosexual activity as intrinsically evil independent of the actor's condition and his social laws and customs.

The Old Testament Context

Because of his Jewish background Paul obviously found the rampant homosexuality he observed in Greece very shocking.

His main point was always that the prevalance of homosexual activity was a sign of alienation from God. He obviously had in mind the Old Testament prohibition of homosexual activity. Consequently, we must note the context of the texts within the Old Testament in which the question of homosexual activity is treated. Homosexual activity was definitely connected in Jewish consciousness with idolatry. An example of this is to be found in Deuteronomy 23:17:

> None of the Israelite women shall become a temple-prostitute, nor shall any of the Israelite men become a temple-prostitute. You shall never bring the gains of a harlot or the earnings of a male prostitute as a votive offering to the temple of the Lord your God; for both are abominable to the Lord your God.

It was a practice among some of Israel's neighbors to use both sexes as part of the fertility rites in temple services. Since the Gods were understood as sexual, they were to be worshiped in overt sexual acts. Whenever homosexual activity is mentioned in the Old Testament, the author usually has in mind the use male worshipers made of male prostitutes provided by the temple authorities.

Paul was well aware of this context from the Old Testament. In reading Paul, it is important to keep in mind what Thielicke refers to as Paul's "central concern" in the text dealing with homosexual activity, especially Romans 1:26. Paul obviously believed that homosexual activity, as far as he understood it, was the result of idolatry. As Wood points out, one must remember the sequence of events as Paul portrays them in Romans.[47] One is not idolatrous because he is a homosexual; he is, however, involved in homosexual activities because he is idolatrous. God punished the idolater by delivering him over to his selfishness and passions. It would appear, then, that Paul treats of homosexual activities only within the context of idol worship. The Holiness Code (Lev. 18:22, 20:13) originally established the connection between idolatry and homosexual activity. The Code specifically warns the Israelites against accepting the idolatrous practices of the Canaanites. One of the provisions of the Code is that homosexual activity is punishable by death.

Several other cultural and historical circumstances ought also to be considered. One must keep in mind the pro-fertility bent of the Old Testament authors due to underpopulation, with the result that any willful destruction of viable human seed was regarded as a serious crime. Another factor influencing the Old Testament attitude on homosexual activity was the strong Hebrew stress on preserving the family name through progeny. In fact, participation in God's covenant with the chosen people depended on having children. One of the worst curses which could befall a Jewish male was that of sterility.

Still another contextual factor has to do with the common use in biblical times of the act of sodomy as an expression of domination, contempt, and scorn. According to J. Edgar Brun, the ultimate "why" of the wrongness of homosexual activity in Israelite eyes can best be discerned in the account of Noah and his sons after the flood (Gen. 9:18-27). The second part of the story has obviously been expurgated and revised. The Hebrew makes it quite clear that Ham did not merely look at his father but actually did something to him. Yet whereas Ham is the wrongdoer, Canaan, his son, is the person cursed. Brun believes the story was undoubtedly an anti-Egyptian polemic and searches to reconstruct it with an episode in the Egyptian epic entitled *The Contending of Horus and Seth* (XI:3–4).

Horus was the posthumous son and heir of the god Osiris, the primordial king and giver of life. He was invited by his uncle, Seth, to spend a day. Seth's real motive was not to show him hospitality but to disqualify him from inheriting his father's royal power. To this end, while Horus slept Seth committed an act of sodomy upon him. Since sodomy was inflicted as a punishment on a defeated enemy and was a symbol of domination, Seth could then claim that he had conquered Horus and demand the kingship in his place. Brun claims that the original biblical story followed the same line: "By committing sodomy upon his father, who was the ancestor of all men after the flood . . . Ham (Egypt) could also claim the right to dominate all mankind."[48] The revision, which omits any explicit reference to a sexual act and makes Canaan the recipient of Noah's curse, was prompted by the fact that the Canaanites had become the immediate threat to Israel's political and religious survival.

Calling attention then to the common practice, especially of the Egyptians, of inflicting sodomy as a punishment upon a defeated male enemy as a symbol of domination, Brun suggests that the principal reason the Israelites regarded homosexual practices as an abomination was that

> they too viewed sodomy as an expression of scorn; and in a society where the dignity of the male was a primary consideration, voluntary acts of a homosexual nature could not be tolerated. Both parties would then be undermining the very foundations of a patriarchal society; the one because he uses another as a woman; the other because he allows himself to be used as a woman. The dignity of the male is dishonored by both.[49]

We have already seen McKenzie's comment that one of the aims of the narrator of the crime of Gibeah was to establish the absolute dignity of the male. It is interesting to note that the Holiness Code only condemns male homosexuality; no mention is made of female homosexual practices, but there is a condemnation under penalty of death of any woman who has sexual relations with an animal.

As Herman van de Spijker notes in his summary of biblical

teaching concerning homosexual activities: both in the Old and the New Testaments, wherever the Bible clearly seems to refer to homosexual activity, we must recognize a judgment of condemnation. However, every text dealing with homosexual activity also refers to aggravating circumstances such as idolatry, sacred prostitution, promiscuity, violent rape, seduction of children, and violation of guests' rights. As a result one can never be sure to what extent the condemnation is of homosexual activities as such or only of homosexual activities under these circumstances: "Nowhere is there a specific text which explicitly rejects all homosexual activities as such independent of the circumstances." Van de Spijker is nevertheless of the opinion that such an objective universal condemnation can be deduced from these texts taken in conjunction with the biblical image of mankind in the creation account of Genesis; he concludes that "all homosexual relationships, even when they are true expressions of an I-thou relationship, are *objectively* contrary to nature as the order of creation."[50]

The Creation Account in Genesis

There are two accounts in Genesis of the creation of human sexuality. The first account, a version dated around 550–500 B.C., is from the Priestly tradition: "So God created man in his own image, in the image of God he created him, male and female he created them." This account clearly indicates that the divine purpose in creating sexual differentiation was procreation. Consequently, the first covenant between God and humanity was a procreative covenant. "And God blessed them and said to them: 'Be fruitful and multiply, and fill the earth and subdue it. . . .'"

However, according to scholars the second account, attributed to the Yahwist author, is much more ancient, dated 950 B.C. In this account God's purpose in creating sexual differentiation is not associated with procreation; rather, the purpose was companionship and a cure for loneliness: "Then the Lord God said, 'It is not good that the man should be alone; I will make him a helper fit for him.'" Thus mutual love and fulfillment is equally a biblical norm for human sexuality. Many moralists seem to ignore the significance of the Yahwist's account of creation and assume that procreation is the only biblical norm.

There is, then, another and, perhaps, more important reason apart from individual texts why some moralists believe that all homosexual activity is condemned in Scripture as contrary to the will of God for man. This reason has to do with the interpretation they give to the creation account in Genesis. As Neale Secor argues, many Christian ethicists read a condemnation of all homosexual activity into the texts dealing specifically with that question because they are reading these particular texts with a basic assumption. The assumption is that the homosexual condition is the result of man's fall and is a deviation from the God-willed state of heterosexuality as expressed in the creation. Under this assumption sexual differentiation is not only normative for human relations; it assumes a metaphysical significance in the very constitution of what is essentially human. "To be human becomes by hypothesis to be purely male or female. Only in monogamous marriage desirous of reproduction is this essential duality held in balance."[51] In the Priestly tradition in the Old Testament, the human male apart from the human female was not considered a full human being. As Rabbi El'azar put it: "Any Jew who has no wife is no man."[52]

Curran appears to be in agreement with this position. As he sees it, human sexuality derives its meaning exclusively "in terms of a relationship of male and female in a procreative union of love."[53] To defend this position he makes a general appeal to scriptural data. "The scriptural data undoubtedly points in this direction, even to the possible extent that the likeness to God is precisely in terms of the sexuality by which men and women are able to enter into a covenant of love with one another." In the opinion of Karl Barth, "man and woman—in the relationship conditioned by this irreversible order—are the human creatures of God and as such the image of God and likeness of the covenant of grace."[54] Since man's likeness to God is to be found in his power to love, some moralists find it necessary to read into that love relationship the specific reality of heterosexual love, almost to the exclusion of all other forms of human community and human love. They tend to identify the biblical concept of person with heterosexual orientation and find in that orientation the divine image in man.

In contrast with this understanding of the scriptural data is T. C. DeKruijf's study, *The Bible on Sexuality*. DeKruijf concludes his survey of Old Testament texts concerning sexual morality by pointing out that the primary message of the Old Testament concerning sexual morality was that love, including sexual love, requires respect for the other person; and the sin which man can commit in his sexual conduct with another consists in dishonoring the person of a fellow human being. "If one does not acknowledge the only true personal God, it follows unavoidably that one will also not acknowledge one's fellow man as a person who has a value of his own."[55] As we have seen, J. Edgar Brun found an identical reason for the condemnation of homosexual activities, since in the cultural and historical context of the Old Testament such activities could only be envisaged as expressions of hatred and scorn. The essential evil of homosexual activities appeared to be the dishonoring of a fellow human being.

DeKruijf points out, however, a very important difference between the treatment of sexuality in the Old and the New Testament. Marriage no longer plays the same role in the New Testament that it did in the Old. In the Old Testament "contact with God was connected with their being the people of God, because in this chosen people God dealt with man. Therefore it was important for every man and woman in Israel to receive this life and pass it on in marriage."[56] To understand the difference of viewpoint in the New Testament it is important to remember that the new people of God are no longer bound by blood relationship; membership in the new people of God is no longer a question of human descent. Consequently, marriage no longer occupies the central place it had in Israel. "In the New Covenant it is given to anyone to be fertile in the new people of God through a love which surpasses even marital love in value and therefore in fertility."[57] This new understanding of love lies at the origin of other vocational choices besides marriage, such as a life of sexual abstinence, and other forms of human community, such as the celibate community. One can no longer identify the love between humans that makes them the likeness of God univocally with the heterosexual relationship in marriage.

Another important difference between the Old and New Testaments concerning human sexuality has to do with the belief in personal immortality. For the most part in the Old Testament there was little stress on personal immortality; rather, stress was placed on the survival of the "people" and one's own survival in and through one's children. However, the New Testament emphasis on resurrection carried with it the belief in personal immortality and, consequently, freed the individual from the necessity of marrying and bearing children in order to achieve a form of survival beyond the grave. This change of emphasis is of particular interest vis à vis the homosexual, since, as many psychologists point out, one of the most profound roots of homophobia is the connection, unconscious for the most part, between homosexuality, barrenness, and death.

Nowhere is this new attitude concerning human sexuality

more evident than in the account of the baptism of the Ethiopian eunuch in the Acts of the Apostles (8:26–39). The
Lucan author had as his purpose to depict the work of the
Holy Spirit in the formation of the first Christian community
and how that community differed from its predecessor. He
stresses that people who were considered outcasts by Israel
for various reasons were to be included in the new community.
The first group are the Samaritans. The second group, symbolized by the eunuch, are those who for sexual reasons were
excluded from the Old Testament community. "No one who
has had his testicles crushed or his penis cut off shall marry
into the Lord's community" (Deut. 23:1). However, in Isaiah
56:2–8 there is an explicit prophecy that with the coming of
the Messiah and the establishment of the new covenant the
eunuch, who was formerly excluded from the community of
God, will be given a special place in the Lord's house and an
immortal value:

> Let not the foreigner who has joined himself to the Lord say:
> "The Lord will surely separate me from his people"; and let not
> the eunuch say: "Behold, I am a dry tree." For thus says the
> Lord: "To the eunuchs who keep my sabbaths, who choose the
> things that please me, and hold fast my covenant, I will give in
> my house and within my walls a monument and a name better
> than sons and daughters; I will give them an everlasting name
> which shall not be cut off . . . these I will bring to my holy moun-
> tain, and make them joyful in my house of prayer; their burnt
> offerings and their sacrifices will be accepted on my altar; for
> my house shall be called a house of prayer for all peoples." Thus
> says the Lord God, who gathers the outcasts of Israel; I will
> gather yet others to him besides those already gathered.[58]

The application of this prophecy to the homosexual can be
defended, because the term "eunuch" in the New Testament
is used not only in its literal sense—i.e., those who have been
physically castrated—but also in a symbolic sense for all those

who for various reasons do not marry and bear children. For example, in Matthew 19:12 Jesus, discussing marriage and divorce, says to his apostles: "There are eunuchs who have been so from birth, and there are eunuchs who have been made eunuchs by men, and there are eunuchs who have made themselves eunuchs for the sake of the kingdom of heaven."[59]

The first category—those eunuchs who have been so from birth—is the closest description we have in the Bible of what we understand today as a homosexual. It should come as no surprise, then, that the first group of outcasts of Israel that the Holy Spirit includes within the new covenant community is symbolized by the Ethiopian eunuch. It is the Spirit who takes the initiative by leading Philip to the encounter with the Ethiopian eunuch of the court of Candace. The eunuch believes in Christ as the Messiah and receives baptism and the Spirit and rides on into history "full of joy." The symbolism of the passage is quite obvious. The Holy Spirit takes the initiative in leading the new Christian community to include among its members those who were excluded for sexual reasons from the Old Testament community.

Later, when we consider natural law ethics, we will also consider whether, in the light of recent psycho-sexual discoveries, heterosexual images of what it means to be a man or a woman derived from the Bible can be uncritically accepted as God-given aspects of creation or whether it must be determined to what extent they are human creations open to serious theological criticism and possible change and development. We can conclude at this point, however, that a general consideration of human sexuality in the Bible leads to only one certain conclusion: those sexual relations can be justified morally which are a true expression of human love. Consequently, once all the cultural and historical circumstances are kept in mind, the only condemnation of homosexual activity to be found with certainty in Scripture is a condemnation of perverse homosexual activity indulged in by otherwise truly heterosexual individuals as an expression of contempt or self-centered lust and usually associated with some form of idol worship. In the Old Testament an attempt was made to desacralize human sexuality by removing it from the realm of the mysterious and impersonal forces of nature. In the New Testament an attempt was made to resacralize human sexuality by integrating it into the ideal context of free, interpersonal human love.

The positive ideal concerning the use of human sexuality proposed in the New Testament is the need all human beings are under to struggle to integrate their sexual powers into their total personality, so that their sexual drive can be totally at the disposition of their desire to achieve union in love with their fellow human beings and with God. There is a considerable body of evidence—the Hooker, Shofield and Weinberg and Williams studies, for example, which we will discuss further on—that many homosexuals have avoided the traps of promiscuity and depersonalized sex by entering into mature homosexual relationships with one partner with the intention of fidelity and mutual support.[60] By means of this relationship they have not only escaped promiscuity but have grown as human beings. They have learned to integrate their sexual powers in a positive way into their personality, with the result that these impulses become no longer a negative, compulsive and destructive force, but an instrument within their control for the expression of human love. There does not seem to be a clear condemnation of such a relationship in Scripture; yet under these circumstances a homosexual relationship could possibly be interpreted as fulfilling the positive ideals of Scripture.[61]

Tradition and Homosexuality

The Appeal to Tradition

Many moralists buttress their claim to found the objective sinfulness of homosexuality on scriptural data with an appeal to tradition. "The Christian tradition has constantly accepted the view that homosexuality goes against the Christian understanding of human sexuality and its meaning."[62] While admitting that historical circumstances and methodological shortcomings have possibly led tradition into error on certain points, yet, Curran concludes, "there seems to be no sufficient evidence for such a judgment in the case of homosexuality." The natural law approach proposed by Aquinas "still seems to correspond to a certain human connaturality condemning homosexuality as wrong."[63] This "human connaturality" might be just that, but it is even more likely that it might be a cultural prejudice formed and fed by tradition itself. In fact, one can and should ask all the same critical questions of tradition that have been previously asked of the scriptural data, especially since that tradition had its primary origin in the scriptural data.

There are three principal sources to which explicit appeal

is made in Western Christian tradition in support of its condemnation of homosexual practices. The first is the contrast in cultural mores between Greek and Hebrew culture. The early Christian community, primarily drawn from among the Jews of the diaspora, were inclined to see any variation of behavior in Greek culture as a deviation from the divine law given to Israel and as the inevitable breakdown of morality due to idolatrous practices. The second major source of the condemnation of homosexual practices was an appeal to the popular Stoic philosophical concept of nature, a concept which culminated in Aquinas's version of natural law. The third source, and in some respects the most important, since it was deemed to be a divine confirmation of the first and second sources, was the prevalent version of the Sodom and Gomorrah story. Let us begin our critical reflection on tradition with this third source.

The Homosexual Interpretation of the Sodom Story

As we have seen, the sin of Sodom was never interpreted in Old Testament times as being primarily sexual, to say nothing of involving homosexual practices; rather it is portrayed as a sin of pride and inhospitality. The first references to the sin of Sodom which indicate explicitly that that sin was of a sexual nature occur in the Palestinian apocrypha of the second century before Christ. In the *Book of Jubilees* XVI.5–6 we read:

> . . . the Lord executed his judgment on Sodom, and Gomorrah and Zeboim, and all the region of the Jordan, and he burned them with fire and brimstone, and destroyed them until this day, even as (lo) I have declared unto thee all their works, that they were wicked and sinners exceedingly, and that they defiled themselves and committed fornication in their flesh, and worked uncleanness on the earth. And in like manner God will execute judgment on the places where they have done accordingly to the uncleanness of the Sodomites, like unto the judgment of Sodom.[64]

In a later passage in the *Book of Jubilees* (XX.5–6) an interesting parallel is drawn between the sin of the Sodomites and the sin of the giants:

> . . . and [Abraham] told [his sons and grandsons] of the judgment of the giants, and the judgment of the Sodomites, how they had been judged on account of their wickedness, and had died on account of their fornication, and uncleaness, and mutual corruption through fornication.

The giants referred to here are the "sons of God" referred to in Gen. 6:1–4 and the "angels" of 2 Peter 2:4 and Jude 6. The "Watchers" of Jewish legend (*Enoch* VI–X; *Jub.* VII.21f., X.5f.; *Test. Reub.* V.6–7; *Test. Naph.* III.5) are represented as lusting after mortal women and descending on earth to enjoy coitus with them. In the *Book of Jubilees* VII.20–22 we read:

> Noah exhorted his sons to . . . guard their soul from fornication and uncleanness and all iniquity. For owing to these things came the flood upon the earth, namely, owing to the fornication wherein the Watchers against the law of their ordinances went a-whoring after the daughters of men, and took themselves wives of all which they chose; and they made the beginnings of uncleanness.

It was from this unlawful intercourse that the Naphidim, or Giants, were born. The *Book of Jubilees* thus draws a parallel between two occasions when illicit sexual conduct called forth the vengeance of the almighty. These passages represent the first departure from the general tradition of Scripture by stressing the sexual character of the sin of Sodom; but that sin is still not indicated as homosexual in nature; rather, it is heterosexual and consisted in the commission of adultery and acts of gross sexual license and shameless promiscuity between men and women. As we have seen, some experts believe that both the scriptural passage dealing with Noah and the flood and the passage dealing with Lot and the rain of fire contain material from the Priestly tradition attacking ancient idolatrous practices concerned with seeking rain, practices which involved sexual orgies.

In a contemporary document, *The Testament of Naphtali* II.4–5, one of the *Testaments of the Twelve Patriarchs*, a Palestinian work of Pharisaic origin, we have the first indication of the sin of Sodom as homosexual in nature:

> . . . recognizing . . . in all created things, the Lord who made all things, that ye become not as Sodom, which changed the order of nature. In like manner the Watchers also changed the order of their nature, whom the Lord cursed at the flood. . . .

Here the offense of both the Watchers and the Sodomites is said to have consisted in changing the "order of nature." Both committed a similar breach of a universal principle of order established by the Creator. The Watchers subverted the natural and evident order by the unlawful mingling in coitus of two incongruous elements, the angelic and the human. If we recall that in the Sodom story the visitors were angels, then the chief offense seems to be understood as a searching for unlawful commerce with an incompatible order of beings, whereas the sexual element is subsidiary in the mind of the author. This interpretation is supported by a New Testament passage, Jude 6–7, in which the evidence of these apocryphal texts can be detected:

> . . . and angels which kept not their own principality, but left their proper habitation, he hath kept in everlasting bonds under darkness unto the judgment of the great day. Even as Sodom and Gomorrah, and the cities about them, having in like manner with these given themselves also to fornication and gone after strange flesh (*hetera sarx*), are set forth as examples suffering the punishment of eternal fire.

Once again the homosexual element is only incidental; the

emphasis is upon the sexual incompatibility of the angelic and human orders rather than upon any particular type of coitus between persons of the same sex. Bailey concludes from this evidence that by the end of the first century A.D., though the sin of Sodom is still regarded as a transgression of order, there is also a perceptible emphasis of its homosexual implications. However, as the *Testament of Naphtali* gives evidence, this development began as early as the second century B.C. The concept of transgression of order adds a new element in a polemical addition to the *Testaments* during the period 70–40 B.C.: ". . . and the daughters of the Gentiles shall ye take to wife, purifying them with an unlawful purification; and your union shall be like unto Sodom and Gomorrah." The reference here is to the mixed marriages so much abhorred by strict Jews. Since Sodom had also come to be associated with barrenness, the passage probably implies that union with Gentile women contracted in defiance of the law will be cursed with sterility.

The next step in this development can be traced to the "writing of Enoch," a lost work written in Hebrew. In the *Testament of Naphtali* IV.1, we find this reference: "I have read in the writings of Enoch ye yourselves also shall depart from the Lord, walking according to all lawlessness of the Gentiles, and ye shall do according to all the wickedness of Sodom." R. H. Charles regards this passage as a loose adaptation of a passage from the *Book of the Secrets of Enoch,* a Hellenistic Jewish work based on the *Writings of Enoch.*[65] In *2 Enoch* XXXIV.2, among the lawless actions of the Gentiles is clearly indicated that of homosexual practices. Consequently by approximately 50 B.C. the interpreters of the *Testaments of the Twelve Patriarchs* began to regard the sin of Sodom as including homosexual practices. The clear connection that the *Testament of Naphtali* V.1 establishes between the "wickedness of Sodom" and the "wickedness of the Gentiles" is significant. This lends support to the possibility that the origin of the homosexual interpretation of the Sodom story can be explained by the Jewish reaction to a closer acquaintance with homosexual practices common in the Hellenistic world during the century preceding the Christian era.

Another passage from a later stratum of 2 Enoch explicitly identifies the sin of Sodom with the pederasty of Hellenic society: "This place [the north region of the third heaven] is prepared for those who dishonor God, who on earth practice the sin against nature, which is child-corruption after the Sodomitic fashion . . . ." However, the first writings to identify the sin of Sodom with homosexual practices in general—the writings which probably had the most decisive influence on early Western Christian tradition—were those of Philo, dating from the middle of the first century A.D., and those of Josephus, from around the year 96 A.D. The first recorded instance of a homosexual coital connotation being clearly attributed to the Hebrew word *yādhá* in the text from Genesis occurs in Philo's *Quaest. et Salut. in Genesis* IV.31–37, where *yādhá* or *suggignomai* is interpreted as "servile, lawless and unseemly pederasty." The association of the wickedness of Sodom with the lawlessness of the Gentiles has become particularly associated with the pederasty of an alien and hostile culture.

In his work *De Abrahamo*, Philo reads all the evils of first-century Alexandria back into the story of Sodom in Genesis:

> The land of the Sodomites was brimful of innumerable iniquities, particularly such as arise from gluttony and lewdness. . . . The inhabitants owed this extreme license to the never-failing lavishness of their sources of wealth. . . . Incapable of bearing such satiety . . . they threw off from their necks the law of nature, and applied themselves to deep drinking of strong liquor and dainty feeding and forbidden forms of intercourse. Not only in their mad lust for women did they violate the marriages of their neighbors,

but also men mounted males without respect for the sex nature which the active partner shares with the passive, and so when they tried to beget children they were discovered to be incapable of any but a sterile seed. Yet the discovery availed them not, so much stronger was the force of their lust which mastered them, as little by little they accustomed those who were by nature men to play the part of women, they saddled them with the formidable curse of a female disease. For not only did they emasculate their bodies, but they worked a further degeneration in their souls, and, so far as in them lay, were corrupting the whole of mankind.[66]

Most of the most prevalent myths and prejudices concerning homosexuality find expression here, such as the myth of effeminacy—the idea that homosexuals must either play the active-masculine role or the passive-feminine role in their relationships—the myth of corruption, and the myth of child abuse. Philo probably did not invent these myths but, as Bailey points out, was only expressing in vivid language a conception of Sodom and its offense which had gradually established itself among Jews of the diaspora during the preceding two centuries of their contact with Hellenic society.

In his *Antiquities* Josephus also clearly identifies the sin of Sodom with homosexual practices, and in particular with pederasty:

About this time the Sodomites were proud on account of their riches and great wealth; they became unjust toward men and impious toward God. . . . They hated strangers, and abused themselves with Sodomitical practices. God was, therefore, much displeased with them, and determined to punish them for their pride.

This passage represents the first clear use of the word sodomy to describe homosexual practices. In still another passage from Josephus' *Antiquities* we read: "Now when the Sodomites saw the young men [the angels] to be of beautiful countenance,

and this to an extraordinary degree . . . they resolved themselves to enjoy these beautiful boys by force and violence."

Although there is good grounds to believe that by the end
of the first century A.D. the sin of Sodom had become widely
identified, among the Jews of the diaspora, with homosexual
practices, yet it is remarkable to note that rabbinical writings
reflect scarcely anything of this development. The majority
of the references to Sodom both in the *Talmud* and the
Midrashim continue to stress the Old Testament themes of
pride, arrogance, and inhospitality. The one exception to this
is a midrash on Genesis: "The Sodomites made an agreement
among themselves whenever a stranger visited them they
should force him to sodomy and rob him of his money."[67]
The writer implies that the most serious and reprehensible
feature of the Sodomite's inhospitality was homosexual acts
reserved for strangers and accompanied by violence and
robbery.

When we turn to the Fathers of the Christian Church,
there is no doubt whatever that they accepted without question
that the sin of the Sodomites was their particular and inordinate addiction to homosexual practices, particularly pederasty, and it was for this reason that God punished them.
Clement of Alexandria, for example, writes that the Sodomites
had "through much luxury fallen into uncleanness, practicing
adultery shamelessly and burning with insane love for boys."[68]
John Chrysostom, in a homily to the people of Antioch, writes:
"The very nature of the punishment was a pattern of the
nature of the sin. Even as [the Sodomites] devised a barren
coitus, not having for its end the procreation of children, so
did God bring on them such a punishment as made the womb
of the land for ever barren and destitute of all fruit."[69] Augustine in his *City of God* speaks of Sodom as "the impious
city where custom had made sodomy as prevalent as laws
have elsewhere made other kinds of wickedness."[70] In another

work Augustine repeats Paul's theme in the Epistle to the Romans that homosexual perversion is itself a recompense for other offenses, since such acts are not only sins per se but also the penalties for sins. In the *Apostolic Constitution* we read: "Thou shalt not corrupt boys: for this wickedness is contrary to nature and arose from Sodom."[71] We should note a second factor entering into the picture with the writings of the Fathers, namely, the Stoic concept of sexual nature with its emphasis on procreation, leading to the judgment that homosexual practices were "contrary to nature." We shall deal with Stoic influences on Christian tradition later on.

Herman van de Spijker summarizes his study of the attitude of the Fathers of the Church on the subject of homosexuality with these words:

> The Fathers consistently rejected homosexual activity. The argument for this rejection was based on the order of creation and the Epistle to the Romans. Sodom is the cautionary example of the punishment to be expected or the clear sign of the lawlessness of such activity. . . . Although the fierceness of the condemnation can be better understood in terms of anti-Hellenic and apologetic motives, and although the Fathers speak mostly against the lust of pederasty and of perverted and self-perverting heterosexuals, yet implicitly they condemn all homosexual activity as contrary to the order of creation. We can conclude from both the biblical and the patristic heterosexual image of man that the Fathers had no understanding of the difference between homosexuality as a subjectively moral expression of love or as an egotistical expression of lust.[72]

The Development of Legal Tradition

A survey of Western Christian tradition concerning homosexual practices would be incomplete without a consideration of the treatment of these practices in Roman law, especially in the codifications of the Christian emperors Theodosius and Justinian, since these codifications exercised a very strong influence not only upon Western European systems of civil and criminal jurisprudence but also upon ecclesiastical law.

The *Lex Scantania* was the original Roman law directed against pederasty, but little is known about it. The next legal measure was the Emperor Philip's law (A.D. 249) abolishing male prostitution. The *Lex Julia de adulteris* (c. 17 B.C.) was probably extended by an interpretive process to include sexual acts committed with boys, a crime meriting capital punishment. For we read that on 30 December 533 the following law was included among the *Institutes* compiled by Tribonian at the Emperor Justinian's request:

> In criminal prosecutions cases, public prosecutions take place under various statutes including the *Lex Julia de adulteris*, . . . which punishes with death (*gladio*) not only those who violate marriages of others, but those who commit acts of vile lust with [other] men.[73]

Thus Roman law was extended to include homosexual acts of all kinds, including those between consenting adults, and the death penalty was assigned.

The first law under the Christian emperors was promulgated on 16 December 342 by Constantius and Constans:

> When a man marries [and is] about to offer [himself] to men in a womanly fashion, what does he wish, when sex has lost its significance; when the crime is one which is not profitable to know; when Venus is changed into another form; when love is sought and not found? We order the statutes to arise, the laws to be armed with an avenging sword, that those infamous persons who are now, or who hereafter may be, guilty may be subjected to exquisite punishment.[74]

As Bailey remarks, it is difficult to know how seriously to take this edict. W. G. Holmes remarks that its curious phraseology "almost suggests that it was enacted in a spirit of mocking complacency."[75]

Fifty years later, on 6 August 390, another law was put
forth by Valentinian II, Theodosious, and Arcadius:

> All persons who have the shameful custom of condemning a
> man's body, acting the part of a woman's, to the sufferance of
> an alien sex (for they appear not to be different from women)
> shall expiate a crime of this kind in avenging flames.[76]

This law is particularly notable because it prescribed the
penalty of burning, which was the most common criminal
punishment imposed upon Sodomists in the Middle Ages and
has persisted at least nominally in some countries until recent
times.

Bailey was of the opinion that these earlier Roman laws
were never rigidly enforced. For by the year 538 Justinian
found it necessary to publish the first of his *Novellae* against
homosexual acts:

> . . . since certain men, seized by diabolical incitement, practice
> among themselves the most disgraceful lusts and act contrary to
> nature; we enjoin them to take to heart the fear of God and the
> judgment to come, and to abstain from suchlike diabolical and
> unlawful lusts, so that they may not be visited by the just wrath
> of God on account of their impious acts, with the result that
> cities perished with all their inhabitants. For we are taught by the
> Holy Scriptures that because of like impious conduct cities have
> indeed perished, together with the men in them. 1 . . . For be-
> cause of such crimes there are famines, earthquakes, and pesti-
> lences, wherefore we admonish men to abstain from the aforesaid
> unlawful acts, that they may not lose their souls. But if after this
> our admonition any are found persisting in such offences, first,
> they render themselves unworthy of the mercy of God, and then
> they are subjected to the punishment enjoined by the law. 2. For
> we order the most illustrious prefect of the Capital to arrest those
> who persist in the aforesaid lawless and impious acts after they
> have been warned by us, and to inflict on them extreme punish-
> ments, so that the city and state may not come to harm by rea-
> son of such wicked deeds.[77]

The chief motive behind this law is clearly stated. Justinian sees homosexual practices as endangering the state; for they are liable to provoke the vengeance of God in the form of earthquakes, famine, and pestilence. We see here the influence of the homosexual interpretation of the Sodom story. Bailey finds the approximate cause of this legislation in the terrible earthquake and floods which in the year 525 devastated the cities of Edessa, Anazarba, and Pompeiopolis in the East, Corinth and Dyrrachium in Europe, while Antioch was destroyed by fire and inundations. In the year 543 a great plague swept through Constantinople. It was doubtless with this in mind that Justinian took occasion during the following Lent, on 1 March 544, to issue a new novella summoning to repentance those in particular whose homosexual practices might provoke other and possibly more dreadful consequences. In that novella he returns to the theme of Sodom:

> 1. For, instructed by the Holy Scriptures, we know that God brought a just judgment upon those who lived in Sodom, on account of this very madness of intercourse, so that to this very day that land burns with inextinguishable fire. By this God teaches us, in order that by means of this we may avert such an untoward fate. . . . Wherefore it behooves all who desire to fear God to abstain from conduct so base and criminal that we do not find it committed even by brute beasts.[78]

Justinian's treatment of homosexual practices became the *locus classicus* for civil legislation concerning this matter. An illustration of how pervasive and perduring that influence was is to be found in Blackstone's treatment of homosexual practices in his *Commentary on the Laws of England:*

> The crime against nature . . . [is one which] . . . the voice of nature and of reason, and the express law of God, determined to be capital. Of which we have a special instance, long before the Jewish dispensation, by the destruction of two cities by fire from

heaven; so that this is a universal, not merely a provincial, pre-
cept. In the Old Testament the law condemns sodomists (and
possibly other homosexual offenders) to death as perpetrators of
an abomination against the Lord, while in the New Testament
they are denounced as transgressors of the natural order and are
disinherited from the kingdom of God as followers of the vile
practices of the heathens.[79]

The first enactment of a Church council concerning homosexual practices occurred at the Council of Elvira in 305–306.
This decree forbade admission of *stupratores puerorum* to
communion even at death.[80] The decree of the Council of
Ancyra in Asia Minor in 314 was extremely influential on the
Church in the West, since it was frequently cited as authoritative in subsequent conciliar enactments against homosexual
practices. Canon 17 concerns those "who either have been
defiled or commit defilement with animals or males."[81] The
council prescribes a variety of punishments dependent on the
age and marital status of the perpetrator. Males, if married
and over fifty, are to be admitted to communion only at the
point of death. Basil of Nyssa in the year 375 in a letter to
Amphilochius, Bishop of Iconium, writes: "He who is guilty
of unseemliness with males will be under discipline for the
same time as adulterers."[82] Gregory of Nyssa in a canonical
letter to Letoius, Bishop of Melitene (c. 390), explains the
reason for treating sodomists the same as adulterers, namely,
because both combine unlawful pleasures with the infliction
of injury upon another.[83] Basil and Gregory both call for
fifteen years of penitence and exclusion from the sacraments.
In 693 Egica, King of Gothic Spain, in an opening speech to
the Sixteenth Council of Toledo, urged the clergy to address
themselves to curbing homosexual practices, and once again
an implicit appeal was made to the Sodom story: "Among
other matters, see that you determine to extirpate that obscene
crime committed by those who lie with males, whose fearful

conduct defiles the charm of honest living and provokes from heaven the wrath of the supreme judge."[84]

The most extensive set of enactments against homosexual practices during mediaeval times were the canons issued by the Council of Naplouse on 23 January 1120 by Baldwin II, King of Jerusalem, and Garmund, Patriarch of Jerusalem.[85] On that occasion a sermon was preached in which all the ills that had befallen the Kingdom of Jerusalem as well as earthquakes, menacing signs, and the attacks of the Saracens were attributed to evil living. Consequently, the council enacted twenty-five canons against the sins of the flesh, four of which dealt with homosexual practices, and burning was prescribed for the impenitent. By the end of the twelfth century sodomy was a reserved sin which must be referred to the bishop or the pope for absolution.[86]

The penitentials (works on the sacrament of penance originating in the Celtic churches of Ireland and Wales) illustrate how the Church attempted to deal with homosexual practices. Their chief concern was to discriminate as fairly as possible between different kinds of acts according to their nature and circumstances and assign appropriate penances. The use and influence of the penitential spread to England, France, Germany, and even Italy and determined for five centuries the standards according to which penance was administered. The most notable pronouncement on the subject of homosexual practices in the Middle Ages was the *Liber Gomorrhianus* of Peter Damian, addressed in 1051 to Pope Leo IX.[87] In this work Peter inveighs against the practice whereby the penitentials distinguish between types of homosexual acts and assign different penances. In particular he calls for the removal from orders of any cleric found guilty of such acts. Leo's response, *Nos Humanius Agentes,* is chiefly remarkable for its emphasis upon the need for a sense of proportion and a more humane approach to the question of homosexual practices. He rebukes the harsh, unyielding spirit of Peter's work, maintaining that not all those who engage in homosexual acts are equally sinful, and thus not all merit the same ecclesiastical censure. He especially notes that it is not necessary to depose a cleric from orders for this reason, concluding: "And if anyone should dare to criticize or carp at this decree of ours, let him know that *he* is in danger of his orders."[88]

Consequently, as Bailey has demonstrated, the formation of the Western Christian attitude to homosexual practices underwent a cumulative process of development in which many diverse influences played a part, the post-exilic Jewish reinterpretation of the Sodom story, pagan and Christian developments of Roman law, the teaching of the Church Fathers, the legacy of Church councils and synods, the penitential system, and so on. By the end of the thirteenth century, and especially with the writings of Aquinas, that tradition was fully formed. The influence of the homosexual interpretation of the Sodom story is evident in every strand of that development. There was a tendency on the part of civil officials to read into any disaster a divine judgment due to homosexual practices. For example, with regard to the wreck of the *Blanche-Nef* in 1120, in which the heir of Henry I of England perished with a number of young nobles, William of Nangis asserts that this was a divine punishment due to the fact that all were sodomists.[89] At the time of the Albigensian heresy there began a tendency to associate homosexual practices with heresy. Since the Albigensian heresy was also known as the Bulgarian heresy, the word *bougre* became associated with sodomy and remains in our present vocabulary as the word "buggery."[90] Bailey argues that although the Albigensians never advocated homosexual practices, their position that marriage was a state of sin gives some credence to the opinion that they had an easygoing attitude toward other forms of sexual activity. All too often unscrupulous politicians would make use of a charge of homosexual activities in order to defeat their political enemies. But it is notable that the Church itself never imposed capital punishment for this sin; rather, its emphasis was on repentance and rehabilitation. In fact the Church courts, by attempting to retain jurisdiction over this question, tried to protect the accused against the more severe punishments of the civil courts.

The ultimate culmination of legal injustice and persecution of the homosexual community in recent times occurred in Hitler's Germany. In 1936 Heinrich Himmler issued a decree which read: "Just as we today have gone back to the ancient German view on the question of marriages mixing different races, so too in our judgment of homosexuality—a symptom of degeneracy which could destroy our race—we must return to the guiding Nordic principle, extermination of degenerates." Orders were given that all homosexuals had to wear purple triangles in public, just as Jews had to wear a star of David. In 1937 the SS newspaper, *Das Schwarze Korps,* estimated that there were two million homosexuals in Germany and called for their extermination. Himmler gave orders that all homosexuals were to be sent to Level 3 camps—that is, death camps.

No one knows exactly how many homosexuals perished. The Austrian Lutheran Church places the number of homosexuals who died at no less than 220,000, the second largest group after the Jews. However, the injustice and the indignity did not end with the fall of the Nazi regime. After the war all other survivors of the concentration camps were treated generously in the matter of reparations. Homosexuals, however, were told that they were ineligible for compensation, since they were still technically "criminals" under German law. The survivors could not even publicly protest, since they had to keep their homosexual identity secret for fear of further discrimination.[91]

The Anomalies of Tradition

In dealing with tradition, it must not be forgotten that the readily available documents which lend themselves to historical interpretation, such as the Bible, law codes, the enactments of councils, and so on, are really only the surface of that tradition—"the proximate or immediate determinants," as Bailey calls them. Underlying these documents are various deep-rooted socio-psychological factors which have come to conscious awareness only in recent times and still await full and careful examination. Speaking of scriptural tradition, Neale Secor remarks:

> One might continue the corrective process by delving into the rather late times when the Genesis traditions were formed for a greater appreciation of the then cultural needs of the monogamous agrarian family unit, the real fear of Canaanite and other apostate idolatrous sexual-religious practices, the primitive reverence for the semen, and the biological misunderstanding regarding the conception and birth processes.[92]

C. Rattrey Taylor in his book *Sex in History* attempts to bring out some of the culturally conditioned attitudes on sexuality.[93] He finds a universal phenomenon in cultures based on a patriarchal principle. These cultures always tend to combine a strongly subordinationist view of women with a repression and horror of male homosexual practices. Whereas cultures based on a matriarchal principle are inclined to combine an enhancement of the status of women with a relative tolerance for male homosexual practices. Taylor concludes that the tradition of the Christian West has been fundamentally "patrist." This may help to explain certain striking anomalies from an ethical viewpoint in that tradition, anomalies which have affected profoundly our laws and public opinion in regard to homosexual practices.

One of the most remarkable of these anomalies is the almost

complete disregard of lesbianism—sexual acts committed by women with one another—in the various documents we have examined. Although the Holiness Code, for example, explicitly condemns under penalty of death male homosexual practices and female bestiality, no mention is made of female homosexual practices. Apart from a disputed reference to unnatural female acts by Paul in Romans 1:26, there is no reference to female homosexuality in Scripture and scarcely any in all the other documents of tradition.

There is a marked tendency, as we have seen, in all the sources of tradition to condemn sodomy in terms of a man "playing the role of a woman" to another man, or using another man "like a woman." As Bailey remarks, this has been looked upon in tradition as the degradation not so much of human nature as of the male as such.[94] If there is a certain message in the narratives of Sodom and Gomorrah and of the Crime of Gibeah, as McKenzie remarks, it is the belief of the time in the absolute respect that should be shown the male and the relative lack of concern for the female. Or from another perspective, one begins to suspect in a careful reading of the documents of tradition that human nature and maleness were frequently identified emotionally, if not consciously, in the popular mind. To stimulate or encourage or compel another to simulate the passive coital function of the female represented a perversion intolerable for a society organized according to the theory of the essential subordination of woman to man, a society which particularly valued male aggressiveness and dominance. Consequently, as Bailey remarks, a man who acted "like a woman" was treated as one who had betrayed not only himself but his whole sex, dragging his fellow men down with him in his voluntary disgrace.

The premise of male superiority also helps to explain the curious disparity between the moral judgment passed upon heterosexual moral offenses on the one hand and homosexual offenses on the other. There is a tradition of referring to homosexual practices as "the most heinous" of all sins. This tradition seems to take its rise in the Story of Joseph (Gen. 37:2), where Joseph is reported to have brought back a "bad report" of his older brothers to his father. The Vulgate translates the passage as "*accusavitque fratres suos apud crimine pessimo.*" Although there is no basis whatsoever in the Bible for reading into this passage an accusation of homosexual practices, yet the term *crimen pessimum* became associated with these practices.

The tradition of male superiority also helps explain why in the popular view female prostitution, fornication, and even adultery are frequently treated with less contempt than homosexual practices. These immoral actions at least proclaim the essential virility of their perpetrators. Every effort at legal reform concerning male homosexual practices brings forth the irrational contention that male homosexuals do more harm to society than a person who seduces a wife or husband, breaks up a marriage, assaults or injures a young girl, begets and abandons an illegitimate child, etc. And the more severe legal penalties testify to the effectiveness of that contention.

Another reason for the distinction traditionally made between male and female homosexual practices is the observation that only male homosexual practices involve the emission of seminal fluid. There has been a definite influence on Western sexual attitudes and on traditional moral theology derived from a reverence for human male semen. This reverence had its origin in an ignorance of human physiology and the conception and birth processes. Because there was no knowledge of the female process of ovulation, women were traditionally believed to be merely the incubators in which male seed was deposited. Clement of Alexandria spoke of the male semen as "*met oligon anthropon*—something almost or about to become a man."[95] The idea that the male semen at emission was almost

human controlled sexual theory until the biological investigations of human physiology in the sixteenth century. Even Galen
spoke of there being no difference between "sowing the womb
and sowing the earth."[96]

Despite the advances in our knowledge of these processes,
the ancient tradition continues to influence our ideas of sexual
conduct and morality until the present day—for example, the
moral attitude to male masturbation. Bailey believes that the
reverence for the male seed as "almost human" was undoubtedly responsible in no small measure for the fact that
society has always tended to reprobate and punish homosexual
practices of males, while more or less ignoring those of females.[97]

Although our ignorance of birth processes has been a thing
of the past for several centuries and the emancipation of
women has made definite strides, something of this deep-seated
but irrational view of women remains today to influence the
attitude of men in general toward the homosexual male. As
we shall see, Dr. George Weinberg believes that the real
psychological crisis in our culture remains male homophobia.[98]
The evidence from tradition suggests an interesting connection
between the status of women and the status of the male homosexual that remains to be explored. Even celibate priests are
frequently themselves victims of an unconscious homophobia.
When John Harvey did a survey of Catholic priests concerning
their attitude toward male homosexuals who might seek their
advice, he discovered:

> Some betrayed an emotional revulsion even to a pastoral discus-
> sion of inversion, quoting St. Paul that such things should not be
> mentioned among us. Others dismissed the subject with an
> abrupt declaration that nothing can be done for inverts and the
> writer was wasting his time. Still others assumed a harsh attitude
> of bitter condemnation.[99]

The lesbian's practices, on the other hand, do not involve any lowering of a privileged social or personal status. Consequently, they can be relatively ignored by a society in some respects fundamentally anthropocentric and homophobic. Bailey concludes:

> It might perhaps be well for us frankly to face the fact that rationalization of sexual prejudices, animated by false notions of sexual privilege, has played no inconsiderable part in forming the tradition which we have inherited and probably controls opinion and policy today in the matter of homosexuality to a greater extent than is commonly realized.[100]

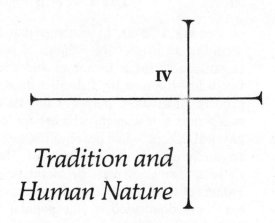

IV

Tradition and Human Nature

The Influence of Stoicism

One important aspect of Western Christian tradition remains to be examined; that is the influence of Stoicism, especially its interpretation of the natural law as regards sexual ethics. Underlying the attitude of the early Church to homosexual practices there was, as we have seen, the belief that they were specially condemned by God in the destruction of Sodom and Gomorrah. Nevertheless, such practices were generally denounced mainly on the grounds that they were in themselves "contrary to nature."

The first such reference to nature, as we have seen, occurred in Paul's Epistle to the Romans. The *Apostolic Constitutions* speaks of ". . . abhoring as unlawful, and that which is practiced by some contrary to nature, as wicked and impious."[101] Tertullian writes: "All other frenzies of lusts which exceed the laws of nature and are impious toward both bodies and the sexes we banish, not only from the threshold, but also from all shelter of the Church, for they are not sins so much as monstrosities."[102] John Chrysostom is particularly emphatic in denouncing homosexual practices as unnatural. Commenting on Romans 1:26–27, he observes that all genuine pleasure is according to nature; the delights of sodomy, however, are an unpardonable insult to nature and doubly destructive. They jeopardize the race by deflecting the sexual organs from their primary procreative purpose, and they sow disharmony between men and women, who are no longer impelled by their physical desires to live peacefully together.[103] Michel Spanneut, an authority on the influence of Stoicism on the Church Fathers, maintains that the moral writings of nearly all the Fathers of the Church in the first two centuries of the Christian era "were dominated by the popular Stoicism of the milieu in which that Christian generation lived."[104]

Stoic philosophy was primarily a moralism. Seneca defined philosophy as "*recta vivendi ratio*."[105] The fundamental Stoic axiom was to "live according to nature." Life according to nature was understood as submission to the divinely appointed order of the world. Nature itself was identified, however, not with instinct but with reason: "To the rational animal the same act is according to nature and according to reason."[106] God, in Stoic philosophy, was understood as reason, or *logos*, diffused through the cosmos. Reason, as "soul of the world," was given a definite biological interpretation. The law of nature was identified with the biological laws governing the physical universe. Thus the rational law of nature represented God's material presence in the universe as cosmic biological reason. To conform to the physical laws of nature was simultaneously to achieve union with the divine. "Live with the gods. And he lives with the gods whoever presents to them his soul accepting their dispensations and busied about the will of God, even that particle of Zeus, which Zeus gives to every man for his controller and governor—to wit, his mind and reason."[107]

The principal virtue of the wise man was understood as ataraxy, or apathy—a life of indifference. In practice Stoic ethics was largely a fight against the passions or affections. These passions—pleasure, sorrow, desire, and fear—were considered irrational and, consequently, unnatural. All forms of passion, even pity and love, were to be eliminated as irrational. The process of achieving a state of indifference was understood as a process of eliminating the influence of affection on human behavior, so that behavior would be totally controlled by reason and completely independent of all externals, even of other persons.[108] In order to escape chance and its capricious happenings, such as the death of a loved one, man must render himself indifferent to all exterior results of his actions, judging them only in terms of their interior effect, which is to be found in the intention. As Spanneut remarks: "The notion of apathy, applied to God, to Christ, and especially to the Christian, received special emphasis. Baptized from the time of Origen, it was used by all the writers [of the early Christian period], particularly in the treatises on anger, and became the ideal of the monk, the basis of his contemplation."[109] Clement of Alexandria devotes an entire chapter of the *Pedagogue* to the connection between good and reason, evil and irrationality.[110] Many of the Christian martyrs—Justin, for example—quote extensively from Stoic sources concerning the virtue of indifference. The Fathers of the Desert appeal to Stoic indifference as the foundation of asceticism. Basil uses the same theme in his writings concerning monastic asceticism.

Hand in hand with the virtue of indifference, the Stoic philosophers stressed a doctrine of rational determinism, according to which everything that happens in the world happens with an ineluctable necessity. "If the gods have determined about me, they have determined well; for it is not easy to imagine a deity without forethought. And as to doing me harm, why should they have any desire toward that? For what advantage would result to them from this, or to the whole which is the special object of their providence?"[111]

Particular emphasis was placed on the triumph over all fears, especially the fear of death. The Stoics denied the immortality of the individual as such; impersonal reason alone is eternal. Thus the only rational response to death was to become detached from life, including one's own. "Be not perturbed, for all things are according to the universal, and in a little time thou wilt be nobody and nowhere, like Hadrian and Augustine."[112] One should learn to value one's existence rationally; that is, only in terms of the positive contribution one can make to the totality. Since the spirituality of the early Church evolved in response to the needs of the martyr, the emphasis on indifference and triumph over the fear of death received particular emphasis.

Along with stress on mind and reason went a dualistic depreciation of the body, both as the seat of the irrational passions and as the contingent element in man. "*Nam corpus hoc animi pondus ac poena est, premente illo lorgetur, in vinculis est.*"[113] Death is to be welcomed as the release of the mind from the chains of the body.

Seneca advised a daily examination of conscience in which one would tote up all the positive and negative aspects of one's existence precisely in terms of one's being able to make a positive contribution to the totality. The truly wise man will become indifferent to life itself. The day he sees his continuance in existence as more of a negative than a positive value, he will be ready to take his own life. The Stoic hero is pictured as cutting his own veins in a warm bath while discoursing in noble indifference about reason to his admiring friends. Thus Seneca himself, in obedience to Nero's command, opened his veins in A.D. 65.

But to persevere in his indifference, the key point in Stoic doctrine was to "never fall in love," that is, never to form a real attachment to anyone. Marcus Aurelius points out that to fall in love is to open yourself up to every misery and to lose all tranquility of soul; for the lover necessarily desires personal immortality both for his loved one and for himself. But such a desire is irrational. Love for another must only take the form of "love for the virtue of which this person is an example." Similarly, in his treatise on friendship Thomas Aquinas holds: "The happy man will need these virtuous friends inasmuch as he seeks to study the virtuous actions of the good man who is his friend."[114]

Consequently, when the Stoics turn to sexual conduct it should come as no surprise that no consideration whatsoever is given to interpersonal love. Rather, stress is placed on the rational end of sexual activity as this end can be read in the biological laws of nature which are one with the will of God. Accordingly, the only rational motive for undertaking sexual intercourse is procreation. Zeno remarks that "cannibalism, incest, and homosexuality are not wrong in themselves," his reasoning being that moral evil pertains to the human will and intention. These actions become wrong because no purely rational motive can exist for such practices.[115]

Stoicism and the Church Fathers

In order to understand the attitude of the Fathers of the Church toward homosexual activity, we must place it within the context of their attitudes on women and on sexuality in general. The early Fathers of the Church tended to accept Platonic and Stoic body-soul dualism. As Emil Brunner notes: "Through Platonic-Hellenic mysticism the idea penetrated into the early Church that the sexual element as such is something low and unworthy of man . . . an idea which . . . is in absolute opposition to the biblical idea of creation."[116] The Fathers frequently repeat Aristotle's dictum that "the woman is a mutilated male" and agree with his position that the male is by nature superior and the female inferior; the one rules and the other is ruled.[117] There is a tendency to identify the male principle with the soul and the female principle with the body. Woman is naturally subject to man because in man the direction of reason is greater. This went hand in hand with a sexual interpretation of original sin, with Eve symbolizing all women as the evil protagonist.

In fact, St. Augustine went so far as to identify all sexual attraction and pleasure with sin. This is Augustine's portrayal of what sexual intercourse exclusively for the purpose of procreation would have been like before man sinned:

> Without the seductive stimulus of passion, with calmness of mind and with no corrupting of the integrity of the body, the husband would lie upon the bosom of the wife. . . . No wild heat of passion would arouse those parts of the body. . . . The semen would have been introduced into the womb of the wife with the integrity of the female organs being preserved, just as now with the same integrity being preserved, the menstrual flow of blood can be emitted from the womb of a virgin. . . . Thus not the eager desire of lust, but the normal exercise of the will should join the male and female for breeding and conception.[118]

Gregory of Nyssa in his turn, in his work *On the Creation of Man,* accepted the androgyne myth of Plato's *Symposium,* namely, that primal man was bisexual. Gregory believed that the male-female severance was a result of sin and a punishment for sin. As a consequence all sexual desires are a vice and have their origin in corrupted nature. John Scotus Erigena, in the ninth century, accepted Gregory's position that man as the perfect image of God was originally without sexual differentiation and that sin was the cause of the differentiation which ensued.[119] In such a climate of opinion it should come as no surprise that Marcion, for example, should refuse to accept into the Church anyone who refused to renounce all sexual relations permanently.

The purely rational end of sexual behavior, procreation, is continuously stressed by the Church Fathers when they are dealing with sexual morality and marriage. One can clearly see the influence of popular Stoic philosophy in the insistence on reason rather than on the sacramental aspect of marriage. Clement, for example, emphasizes the irrationality of seeking only pleasure in marriage.[120] Justin Martyr reflects popular Stoicism when he writes: "We [Christians] do not enter marriage for any other reason than to have children."[121] Jerome quotes the saying of Sextus with approval: "He who loves his own wife ardently is an adulterer."

Aquinas and Stoicism

Thomas Aquinas was the only great scholastic theologian to discuss the subject of homosexual practices in any detail. Albert the Great, in a short reference, gives four reasons why this is the most detestable of practices: it proceeds from a burning frenzy; it has a disgusting foulness; those addicted to it seldom succeed in shaking off the vice; and, finally, it is as contagious as any disease, rapidly spreading from one to another.[122]

In contrast to that of Albert, Thomas's treatment is calm and dispassionate.[123] As in the case of the Fathers, we must place Thomas's treatment of homosexuality in the context of his treatment of women and of sexuality in general. Woman, he held, was "the inferior workman who prepares the material for the skilled artisan, the male."[124] He theorizes that since every child born should be male, because the effect should resemble its cause, there must be some etiological explanation for the birth of the inferior female. Such a birth, he claims, need not necessarily be the result of some intrinsic factor—a "defect in active power" or an "indisposition of the material"—but may sometimes arise from an extrinsic accident. He quotes the Philosopher (Aristotle) to the effect that "a moist south wind helps in the generation of females, while a brisk north wind helps in the generation of males."[125] Thomas's attitude toward women is best expressed when he says of Eve: "She was not fit to help man except in generation, because another man would have proved more effective help in anything else."[126]

Concerning human sexuality in general, Aquinas rejects John Scotus's position that sexual differentiation as such is due to sin, but he agrees with Augustine's Stoic view that all sexual pleasure is the result of sin.[127] The Stoic influence is evident in the fact that Aquinas deals with the subject of homosexuality in the course of his treatise on the cardinal virtue of temperance. He identifies the vice contrary to this virtue as lust, whose essence is "to exceed the order and mode of reason where venereal acts are concerned." Any act which is not consistent with the proper end of venereal acts, namely the generation and education of children, necessarily pertains to the vice of lust. The lustful man desires not human generation but venereal pleasure, and it should be noted that this pleasure can be experienced by indulging in acts which do not issue in human procreation. It is precisely this which is sought in the sin against nature.[128]

Thus the first grounds for Thomas's condemnation of homosexual practices is his belief that they necessarily represent an inordinate selfish seeking of venereal pleasure; and, as we have seen, Thomas believed that all such pleasure is the result of sin. What we should note with interest is that there is no mention in this passage of a third possible motive for venereal acts, whether heterosexual or homosexual, besides either lust or procreation—namely, the possibility that they might be an expression of genuine interpersonal love. There is no reason to assume that Aquinas had any more awareness than had the Church Fathers of the homosexual condition. Rather, it is almost certain that in his reference to homosexual practices he is assuming that these are merely sexual indulgences undertaken from a motive of lust by otherwise heterosexual persons. This is the conclusion drawn by Joseph McCaffrey in his study

of Aquinas's treatment of homosexuality. Having rigidly subordinated the rational and, therefore, moral use of sex in general to one end—procreation—Aquinas assumes that homosexual
acts, since they cannot serve that purpose, must be motivated
necessarily and exclusively by a drive toward sexual pleasure.

  In a response to an objection that if no one is injured by
homosexual activities, there is no sin against charity, Aquinas
points out that the order of nature is derived from God. Consequently, any contravention of that order is necessarily "an
injury done to the Creator."[129] Thus the most fundamental objection Aquinas had to homosexual practices was identical to
that of the Stoics: they cannot serve the exclusive divine purpose governing the use of all human sexuality, the end of
procreation. It would seem that Aquinas, like his Stoic prede-
cessors, never even considered the possibility that human sexual behavior, even in a heterosexual context, never mind a
homosexual one, could be morally justified as an expression of
human love.

  In one relatively unknown but important passage in his
Summa Theologica, Thomas speaks of homosexual practices
as capable of being *"connaturale secundum quid."*[130] He asks
the question, When is pleasure "according to nature"? He dis-
tinguishes between those pleasures that are according to human nature specifically as rational—such as the "contemplation
of the truth"—and those pleasures which humans have in common with other animals—such as "venereal activity" (*veneorum
usus*). But, he continues: "In the case of both types of pleasure
it can happen that what is unnatural simply speaking can be
connatural in a certain situation. For it can occur that in a
particular individual there can be a breakdown of some natural
principle of the species and thus what is contrary to the nature
of the species can become by accident natural to this individual
(*per accidens naturale huic individuo*)." Among other ex-

amples of this, Thomas explicitly mentions male homosexual activity (*in coitu masculorum*). Unfortunately he never explores this distinction further.

To deal exclusively with the passages in which Aquinas speaks explicitly of homosexual practices is somewhat unjust to his influence upon the consequent development of sexual ethics. Although Aquinas himself did not apply his new insights to practical ethical issues, he did lay the philosophical foundation for a personalist ethics. It was not until he reversed the act-potency relationship of Greek philosophy with his central idea of a real distinction between essence, or nature, as potency and existence as act that a philosophical foundation was laid for understanding man as positively individual and unique and, therefore, incapable of being legitimately totally relativized to the ends of the species from an ethical viewpoint. Further, Thomas opened up the possibility of conceiving human nature not as a static given, but as a dynamic teleological process of growth and development. This made possible an understanding of ethical norms as ideal goals governing the development of personal community, rather than just biological nature. But this development had to await the work of philosophers true to the spirit, if not the letter, of Thomistic philosophy. It was not until the rise of modern personalist philosophies of human subjectivity and freedom that an appropriate methodology for an ethical study of human sexuality in a personalist context became available.

Homosexual Activity and Procreation

Many moral theologians grant that the older Catholic approach to sexual morality inordinately placed all the emphasis on the biological and physical aspects of the sexual act, ignoring the interpersonal context in which the act takes place. "The procreative aspect becomes the primary and sometimes the only purpose of sexuality."[131] However, these same moralists

are of the opinion that one must maintain some connection
between the personal and the procreative aspects of human
sexuality: "The joining together of the love union and procreative aspects does appear to be the meaning of human sexuality
and marriage. There seems to be a strong presumption in
favor of such an understanding which cannot be overturned
without grave reason."[132]

When, therefore, they come to the specific problem of homosexual behavior, these same theologians appeal to this necessary and indissoluble connection between procreation and
human sexuality as another reason for the condemnation of
homosexual activity:

> The position of the hierarchical magisterium in the Roman
> Catholic Church would argue that every single act of sexual inter-
> course must be open to procreation. Obviously, such an approach
> gives one a strong rule and criterion to use in condemning homo-
> sexual acts or other seemingly errant forms of sexual behavior.[133]

This is by no means as obvious a conclusion as many believe. The Church's attitude toward the ends of marriage has
undergone a definite development. Beginning with an early
insistence, under Stoic influence, on the exclusive end of
procreation, at a later stage the Church began to stress procreation as the primary end, but granted the existence of secondary
ends, namely the mutual love and fulfillment of the marriage
partners. The Church has traditionally recognized the moral
goodness of heterosexual relations between a married couple
incapable of having children; this despite the heavy emphasis
of tradition that procreation must be the primary aim of all
sexual activity. For example, Pope Pius XI in his encyclical
Casti Connubii (No. 59) writes:

> Nor are those considered as acting against nature whc in the
> married state use their right [to sexual intercourse] in the
> proper manner, although on account of natural reasons either of

time or of certain defects, new life cannot be brought forth. For
in matrimony as well as in the use of matrimonial rights there are
also secondary ends such as mutual aid, the cultivation of mutual
love and the quieting of concupiscence which husband and wife
are not forbidden to consider as long as they are subordinated to
the primary end and so long as the intrinsic meaning of the act
is preserved.[134]

From the moment the Church granted the morality of the
rhythm method, for example, as a natural form of birth control, and justified sexual activity as still fulfilling the "secondary" aims of mutual love and fulfillment, there was a serious
reason to reconsider the traditional position that all homosexual
activities are necessarily wrong on the ground that they cannot lead to procreation. In a relatively overlooked passage of
this same encyclical, *Casti Connubii*, the mutual love between
the partners is recognized in its own right as the "*primaria
matrimonii causa et ratio*":

> The mutual inward moulding of husband and wife, this deter-
> mined effort to perfect each other, can in a very real sense, as the
> Roman Cathechism teaches, be said to be the chief reason and
> purpose of matrimony, provided matrimony be looked at not in
> the restricted sense as instituted for the proper conception and.
> education of children, but more widely as the blending of life
> as a whole and the mutual interchange and sharing thereof.[135]

In their treatment of marriage in the document Pastoral
Constitution on the Church in the Modern World, the Council
Fathers at Vatican II go a step further in this development by
dropping all reference to primary and secondary ends. As
Robert McAfee Brown comments:

> The document . . . goes far beyond the traditional teaching that
> the procreation and education of children are the primary ends
> of marriage. Thanks to the interventions of such men as Cardi-
> nals Léger and Suenens, the document stresses the importance of
> conjugal love. Sexual love between men and women is clearly

distinguished from "the dispositions of lower forms of life"—
where one has a suspicion it often used to linger in the thought
of earlier moral theologians. Pure conjugal love "involves the
good of the whole person." In such statements the lie is given
to the notion that sex in marriage is evil, or only a concession to
concupiscence, or valid only for procreation.[136]

The Church continues to condemn any voluntary separation
of the coequal purposes of sexual behavior, procreation and
mutual love. However, such an argument against voluntary
separation would be applicable to the homosexual only if one
refuses to accept the psychological data concerning the homosexual condition and persists in viewing all those who involve
themselves in homosexual practices as remaining free to choose
heterosexual relationships. The genuine homosexuals' situation is more comparable factually to that of a heterosexual
couple incapable of having children than, for example, to the
situation of those who practice birth control, since it is not
through a free choice within their control that homosexuals
eliminate the possibility of procreation from their sexual life.
Yet there is a considerable body of evidence that those homosexuals who have limited their sexual expression in an ethically
responsible way have by that means achieved what Pius XI
indicates as the "chief reason and purpose" of sexual love
within marriage looked at in a wider context "as the blending
of life as a whole and the mutual interchange and sharing
thereof."

Human Nature and Homosexuality

One all-important problem remains. Even granting that
mutual love and fulfillment is a coequal natural end of human
sexuality as such, there seems to be a lingering doubt that this
end could possibly justify homosexual activities, since these
activities seem so obviously to involve a perversion of the biological function of the sexual organs. As we have seen, the

phrase "against nature" has retained its meaning from its Stoic origin as "contrary to reason." One learns the purposes of nature by an impersonal and objective reading of the biological law governing the sexual operations of the human body. However, this understanding of nature represented in fact a rejection of what is unique in human nature as such, namely, the personal realm. Consequently, it negates any possibility of understanding human sexual activity within the specifically human dimension of interpersonal love.

Humans emerge from the impersonal forces of nature precisely as self-aware and free. What is specific about human nature is not some quality which is common to all the species, such as reason, but the fact that "every individual is more than the species."[137] It is this personal uniqueness of every individual which forms the necessary basis for the possibility of human love. A loving action, even if it takes the form of a sexual gesture, must be directed to the other as unique, as end in himself or herself. To treat another person merely as a means to an end that lies outside the person himself represents a failure to love that person as unique.

From this personalist viewpoint an overemphasis on procreation can be seen as leading potentially to a seriously immoral and dehumanizing form of sexuality. Modern consciousness has been sensitized by the movement for women's rights to the fact that to understand the female exclusively in a functional manner as "bearer of children" is a depersonalizing and, therefore, immoral attitude. Such an emphasis can be seen as in conflict with the Gospel emphasis on the respect and love due to one's fellow human as person. As we have seen, a general consideration of scriptural data concerning sexual behavior leads to only one certain conclusion: those sexual relations can be justified morally which are a true expression of human love. The call of the Gospel to man is not one of conforming passively to biological givens; rather, that call is to transform and humanize the natural order through the power to love.

The overemphasis on nature, reason, and law in tradition has seriously falsified the moral question of sexual behavior in the minds of many people. The average person has associated and confused the question of the *morality* of sexual conduct with the question of its objective *legal* status. The reason for this confusion is, in part, that one finds a very easily applied objective norm: sex before marriage is wrong; sex after marriage is right. The difficulty of this norm can be easily perceived if we begin with the question of the moral quality of sexual conduct within marriage. The wife who withholds sex with a view to negotiating a fur coat is acting immorally; she is behaving like a prostitute, even if a legal prostitute. And the husband who uses his wife as a convenient instrument of masturbation, seeking exclusively his own egotistical pleasure, is immoral and remains so even if the act is open to the possibility of procreation. From these examples it should be obvious that there is something more to the moral quality of sexual behavior than the purely objective legal question of marriage, or even the objective rational question of openness to procreation. Something else ought to be present; and that something else is love. Are you using your sexual powers as a means of expressing your love? Are you centering your existence in the one you love and seeking his or her fulfillment in what you are doing? The human conforms to the divine image revealed in Christ not by acting in an impersonal, rational way, but by acting from a motive of love.

Human Freedom and Human Sexuality

It is obvious that the traditional moral theologians understood man's sexual behavior as rationally determined by biological instinct. Thus the only freedom they believed man to have in the sexual realm was the freedom to conform to the rational end built into biological instinct, procreation, or to thwart that end. However, we have become progressively aware in recent times that human sexuality, like all human reality precisely as human, participates in the radical freedom of man. In forming their respective judgments, many moralists seem to ignore the rather obvious fact that human sexuality is not a totally instinctive and, therefore, determined phenomenon. Whatever participates in human freedom cannot receive its total explanation in terms of causal determinacy. Rather, it can be adequately understood only in terms of ideal goal or purpose. Man is freed from a deterministic *vis a tergo* precisely because he is able to project ideal goals and, consequently, allow these ideals to be the ultimately determining factor in his behavior.[138]

We do not find it "contrary to nature" that man has taken the hands which biological evolution provided him as grasping instruments and employed them in the ideal creative pursuits of wielding a brush or a pen. Nor do we find it contrary to nature that man has used his mouth with its teeth, tongue and lips, obviously intended by nature for eating, in order to communicate through speech and song his most intimate aspirations. Nor should we find it any less according to nature, if man should use his sexual organs, designed by nature for procreation, in order to give the most intimate expression to his drive for union in love with his fellow man.

How, then, does man's freedom enter into the formation of his sexual orientation? We are born male or female, biologically speaking: but biological givens never determine human behavior precisely as human. We become "men" or "women" through a free human process of education. What it means to be a man or woman in any given society or culture is a free human cultural creation. Every culture has created its ideal sexual-identity images for the masculine or feminine role. Successful cultural adaptation represents the process whereby the young, unconsciously for the most part, adapt themselves to

the prevalent cultural image and expectations which go along
with their biological identity.

More often than not in the past, these cultural identity
images contained seriously dehumanizing factors. It is only
in recent times that humanity has become aware that these
images are not predetermined either by God or nature. As
long as the cultural process remained unconscious there was
little awareness of the role human freedom played in the formation of these images. Because these images were considered
as either divine or psychological givens or taboos and their
true character as free human constructs was not recognized,
there was no hope of liberation from their destructive and
anti-human elements. Primitive cultures tended to sacralize
the prevailing images, seeing them as given by the gods. However, as Thomas Driver convincingly argues in his article
"Sexuality and Jesus," over against the pagan gods and the
pagan religions Jesus appeared as the great neutralizer of the
religious meaning of sex; and, thus, as humanity's liberator
from narrow sexual taboos mistakenly identified as divine im-
peratives:

> I believe that the construction of a Christian ethic of sex cannot
> be properly attempted as long as one retains the mythology of
> sexuality that grew up in the ancient religions, is perpetuated in
> the new ones, and from which Jesus as the Christ would liberate
> us.[139]

Since the sexual-identity image which concretizes heterosexual relations at any point in human history is a human and
not a divine creation, theologians who absolutize the man-
woman relation as the "divine image" in man are guilty of
raising a human creation to the level of an idol. The task of
the theologian, true to the spirit of Jesus in the New Testament, should be to liberate humanity to "the glorious liberty
of the Sons of God," precisely by undertaking a critical theo-

logical investigation of sexual-identity images. As we have seen, the primary God-given ideal goal of human sexual development is that we should fashion cultural identity images that make it possible for human beings to achieve the fullness of a true personal relationship of sexual love in the process of conforming to the images provided by culture.

A growing body of evidence derived from cultural anthropology, sociology, and psychology indicates that in the learning process whereby humans conform to the sexual-identity images of their culture, a certain percentage, approximately one out of ten, fail to acculturate themselves successfully according to the acceptable heterosexual pattern. This appears to be a consistent and universal cultural phenomenon, the same in all cultures and in all periods of history.[140] Since it is the divine plan that humans should freely construct their cultural identity images, and since it seems to be a universal phenomenon that a certain percentage of humans do not necessarily conform to the accepted heterosexual pattern, no matter how heavily conformity to that pattern is sanctioned by society and the Church, I see no reason to assume a priori that the human who emerges from that unconscious learning process as a homosexual is somehow alienated from God's plan or in conflict with nature's design. On the contrary, it would seem more reasonable to assume that the homosexual is part of the divine plan and has an intrinsic role to play in human society. What that role may be will be the object of our inquiry in the second part of this work.

Paul Lehmann, in his work *Ethics in a Christian Context*, makes the point that the concern of a Christian ethics should be to relate the intimate reality of human sexuality in all its forms to the freedom and integrity of human wholeness: "What is called for in Christian sexual ethics is an approach which accents both the fundamental importance of the sexual act for the humanization of man and the setting in which that

humanization of man is a concrete and achievable reality."[141]
Kimball-Jones suggests that for the true homosexual such a
setting can only exist in an encounter with another person of
the same sex. Such an encounter is "the only sexual setting in
which 'the humanization of man' can begin to become 'a concrete and achievable reality' for the homosexual."[142]

Homosexual love, although incapable of procreation, is certainly not doomed to fruitlessness. Many homosexual couples
love, and would gladly adopt, children if the law would permit it. Apart from this, it is certain that by means of a homosexual love many humans have been liberated to a truly spiritual fertility which otherwise would have been impossible. And
as DeKruijf remarks in a different context: "In the New Covenant it is given to anyone to be fertile in the new people of
God through a love which surpasses even marital love in value
and therefore in fertility."[143] We shall treat of the potentially
positive aspects of homosexuality later on. First we must in-
vestigate the contribution of the human sciences to our moral
understanding of homosexuality.

V

The Human Sciences and
Homosexuality

The Use of Scientific Data

As Curran points out, there are two questions concerning
the use of empirical data derived from the human behavioral
sciences: the substantive question, which has to do with a
search for the meaning of homosexuality in terms of the human
sciences such as psychology, sociology, psychiatry, anthropology, cross-cultural studies, etc.; and the methodological question concerning the way in which such data should influence
and be incorporated into moral judgment.

He rejects, on the one hand, the methodological position of
Karl Barth, which would "exclude all human wisdom as helpful to the Christian ethicist, and depends exclusively on revelation."[144] On the other hand, he equally rejects Milhaven's
methodology "of relying exclusively on communal experience
which in this case is preeminently the findings of psychology
and psychiatry."[145] In contrast to Milhaven, Curran emphasizes
the dynamic and progressive character of moral judgment,
which always is concerned with what ought to be in contrast
to the present experience of what is. "Present experience too

easily forgets the prophetic aspect of Christian teaching, which corresponds with an eschatology which negatively criticizes the present in the light of the future."[146]

Since the human experience which enters into ethical judgment must be total, it must relate to the full reality of the world around us, including man's relationship to God and to his fellow man. Such an experience can never be reduced exclusively to the data of the behavioral sciences, since "these scientific disciplines have a perspective which can never be totally identified with the human perspective."[147] The final human moral judgment must be a synthetic and creative judgment which, while incorporating the data of the human sciences, must relativize all these data in terms of the total human perspective.

Granting the value of this methodological statement, the real difficulty arises when we consider the substantive contribution of the human sciences to an understanding of the meaning of human homosexuality. Some moralists believe that a telling argument for the validity of the traditional condemnation of homosexual practices comes from the data of the human sciences, the majority of which, Curran claims, "seem to point to the fact that human sexuality has its proper meaning in terms of the love union of male and female."[148]

What we are witnessing in the writing of many moral theologians, especially in the area of sexual ethics, is a shift in the basis for understanding what constitutes human nature. Whereas, as we have seen, traditional sources based their understanding of sexual nature primarily on an objective biological function, the modern theologian tends to seek his primary evidence for what is true to human nature from psychological and sociological data. Consequently, most modern condemnations of homosexual practices are based in so-called psychological or sociological data.

Promiscuity and Homosexuality

The claim is frequently made on the basis of scientific data that homosexual acts represent a failure in full human development and that homosexual practices are necessarily psychologically destructive for the parties involved. Curran, for example, insists that those who argue in favor of homosexuality "fail to come to grips with the accepted fact that *most* homosexual liaisons are of the 'one night stand' variety." Consequently, there is no sexual union expressive of loving commitment to one another. "No one can deny that there are many stable relationships, but these do not clearly constitute the majority of the cases."[149]

The scientific data that Curran adduces in support of his statement that most homosexual liaisons are promiscuous derive from a reference in a footnote to a sociological study, "Homosexuality: The Formation of a Sociological Perspective," by Simon and Gagnon. He quotes these sociologists as writing: "These data, then, suggest a depersonalized quality, a driven or compulsive character quality, to the sexual activity of many homosexuals, which cannot be reckoned as anything but extremely costly to them."[150] Curran himself acknowledges, however, that there are "many stable homosexual relationships" and lists the authors of a number of recent scientific studies (Clara Thompson, Evelyn Hooker, Wardell Pomeroy, etc.) who indicate the hitherto unsuspected numbers of such successful liaisons.[151]

These same authors establish excellent reasons why these stable liaisons must remain hidden and, consequently, why accurate statistical data concerning the stability of homosexual liaisons is for all practical purposes difficult, if not impossible, to obtain. Thus there can be no certain scientific data to justify a clear conclusion that "stable relationships are not a majority." In view of widespread premarital activity, prostitution, marital infidelity, the increasing divorce rate (which a recent survey claims is rapidly approaching the fifty percent mark), etc., one wonders what specific data could be offered to prove the existence of a lesser degree of infidelity and depersonalized and compulsive sexual activity among heterosexuals. Whenever and by whomever sexual promiscuity is indulged in, one has to do with a neurotic, unhappy, and compulsive form of sexuality. The real moral miracle the data does give witness to is that despite every obstacle that society and the Church have placed in the way of homosexual relationships, many have succeeded in maintaining a high degree of stability and have provided a truly human companionship and fulfillment.

As for the statement "Those who argue in favor of homosexuality have failed to come to grips with the problem of the transitory nature of many homosexual liaisons," just the opposite is the truth.[152] The majority of authors dealing with the problem recognize and establish beyond serious doubt that the primary reason for this negative quality in many homosexual liaisons is the guilt and self-hatred which so many homosexuals tend to introject as a result of the judgment passed on them by society. As Dennis Altman observes:

> Like the black, the homosexual suffers from a self-fulfilling stereotype. Tell people long enough that they are inferior, and they will come to believe it. Most of us are niggers because we believe that we are in large part what society constantly brands us as; in response we come to exhibit the characteristics that justify our stigma. There are a large number of neurotic, unhappy, compulsively promiscuous homosexuals whom one might well regard as "pathological." This pathology is, however, the result of social pressures and the way they have internalized these, not of homosexuality itself. If people are led to feel guilty about an essential part of their own identity, they will in all likelihood experience considerable psychological pressures.[153]

But even if we grant for the sake of argument that the majority of the homosexual's liaisons are promiscuous, this does not establish a rational grounds for the condemnation of homosexuality as such, but only of promiscuity. If it should happen that the data in a given society proved that the majority of heterosexual contacts were of a one-night-stand variety, would the conclusion follow, then, that heterosexual activities in themselves are sinful? Obviously one is assuming some unproven intrinsic connection between homosexuality and promiscuity. The fact remains that if even only one homosexual liaison can be proven to have been an expression of genuine human love and fidelity, then the existence of such an intrinsic necessary connection has been effectively disproven.

It does not take much imagination to understand how much heterosexual activity would tend to be dehumanized and compulsive if heterosexual liaisons were considered illegal and criminal by the state and the effect of sin by the Church. As we have seen, the insistence on the objective sinfulness of all homosexual relationships is precisely the type of moral thinking that psychologically destroys the ability of many homosexuals to enter into a permanent and fruitful relationship. The only certain substantive conclusion that follows from the scientific data is the terrible cost in terms of human suffering and degradation that has followed on the mistaken moral judgments and prejudices of the past which still are invoked to support the prejudices of the present.

Psychiatry and Homosexuality

One school of psychiatrists maintain that homosexuality in all cases represents a mental disease. A proponent of this position is Irving Bieber in his work *Homosexuality: A Psychoanalytic Study*. Isadore Rubin, in a discussion guide for SIECUS, reports that although there is no unanimity among specialists, the most commonly held opinion is that *all* homosexuals are mentally ill or neurotic. Edmund Bergler, in his

book *Homosexuality: Disease or Way of Life,* defines homosexuality as

> a neurotic distortion of the whole personality. . . . There are no
> healthy homosexuals. The entire personality structure of the
> homosexual is pervaded by the unconscious wish to suffer. This
> wish is gratified by self-created trouble-making (psychic maso-
> chism) . . . he is an emotionally sick person.[154]

Many experts challenge this extreme position of some psychiatrists. They point out, first of all, that these men arrive at
their conclusion as a universal judgment, not from experience
but by means of an implicit invalid speculative argument. Assuming the sex drive as such to be the total economic content
of the personality and defining heterosexual adjustment as the
ideal and exclusive goal of unconscious personal development,
they are forced to conclude a priori that all homosexuality represents a fixation at, or regression to, an immature stage of
development. Irving Bieber begins with exactly the same assumption as the natural law ethicians: "We assume that heterosexuality is the *biologic* norm, and that unless interfered with
all individuals are heterosexual."[155] Further, most psychiatrists
tend to deal in the practical order only with those homosexuals
who have severe neurotic disorders or personality conflicts,
and almost never deal with the hidden majority who have
managed more or less to escape severe emotional disturbance
because of their condition. As one expert observed: "When
clinicians speak of homosexuality, they are speaking of a very
particular type of neurotic interaction, rather than a type of
sexual behavior."[156] This observation is borne out by a statement in the introduction to Bergler's book: "All psychoanalytic
theories assume that adult homosexuality is psychopathologic
and assign different weights to constitutional and experiential
components."[157]

Still another, and apparently larger, group of psychiatrists
seem to take a middle position. Freud himself was the first

clinician to suggest that homosexuality as such does not inherently constitute an emotional illness.[158] As Louis Crompton points out:

> When to such names as Freud and Krafft-Ebing, one adds those of Frank Beach, Harry Benjamin, Evelyn Hooker, Wardell Pomeroy, Alfred Kinsey, Robert Lindner, Judd Marmor, Michael Shofield, Thomas Szasz and Ernest van den Haag, as well as the Wolfenden Committee, the most distinguished government group ever to undertake a study of the subject, it is obvious, to say the least, that the sickness theory does not command the universal acceptance in scientific world which many assume it does.[159]

Many authors argue that the emotional disturbances which frequently accompany the homosexual condition are primarily the result of social pressures. These disturbances are usually not found in those cultures where homosexual behavior is socially acceptable.[160]

Still other authors point out that the neurotic traits ascribed to homosexuals are the same for any individual who identifies himself with a persecuted minority. John Cavanaugh concludes his study of this question with the following statement:

1. Homosexuality is not a disease per se.
2. Deviant sexuality, including homosexuality, is the result of a personality or character problem in which the sexual orientation of an individual becomes fixated at an early age.
3. Homosexuality may be a symptom of neurosis or psychosis, but in such cases it represents the individual's reaction to society or society's reaction to the individual.[161]

Kimball-Jones concludes his survey of the various opinions of psychiatrists with this observation:

> While in each of these representative views homosexuality is seen as constituting a *psychiatric abnormality*, it is in no instance seen as inherently constituting a *serious and debilitating mental illness*.[162]

There are experts, however, who challenge the judgment that homosexuality necessarily represents psychiatric abnormality. Wainwright Churchill, for example, points out that there obviously are homosexuals who are homosexuals because of their inter-psychic conflicts. Their homosexuality originates in such conflict and is maintained by it. However, any type of sexual behavior—homosexual, heterosexual or autoerotic—can become associated with psychopathologic trends. When homosexuality is associated with pathology, it tends to become compulsive; the individual tends to use sexuality as a means of coping with anxiety, much as the alcoholic uses alcohol. Churchill contends, however, that clinicians in their diagnosis of *all* homosexuality as psychiatric abnormality have ignored the existence of evidence coming from cross-cultural and cross-species investigations. As one advances in the scale of evolution, sexual behavior progressively loses its instinctual determination and more and more takes on the nature of learned behavior. Among more advanced mammals, homosexual behavior becomes more frequent. Explanations of adult homosexual practices in terms of complexes rooted in various childhood conflicts seem to have little or no applicability to these forms of homosexual behavior:

> To imagine for example that a baboon becomes positively conditioned to homosexual stimuli as a result of a pathological relationship with a "close-binding-intimate" mother or the result of some other complex is little less than ridiculous.[163]

Churchill testifies, however, to the psychological normalcy of many of his homosexual patients:

> This author wishes to go on record as one clinician among a multitude of others who has had the opportunity to interview, and, in several cases, to become acquainted with homosexual males who meet with every reasonable standard of mental health in their relationships with themselves and with others.[164]

Only in recent times has any effort been made to study those individuals who live relatively discreet, stable, law-abiding, constructive, and socially useful lives as homosexuals. Yet it is this group which may, perhaps, constitute the largest proportion of those engaging in homosexual practices. Perhaps the most important study done to date in America on the "well-adjusted" homosexual was that of Evelyn Hooker published in the New York Council of Churches report *Foundations for Christian Family Policy* (1961). Hooker sought out as her research subjects those homosexuals "who did not seek psychiatric help and who led relatively stable, occupationally successful lives." When the results of tests administered to this group were compared to those of tests administered to a like group of heterosexuals, psychologists found great difficulty in determining who were the homosexuals, and in many cases found "no evidence of any demonstrable pathology." Hooker quotes a fellow clinician's conclusions:

> Homosexuality is not a clinical entity, but a symptom with different meanings in different personality set-ups. An overt homosexual way of life can play a constructive or destructive role in the personality. It may be the best type of human relation of which a person is capable, and as such is better than isolation. . . . Or it may be an added destructive touch in a deteriorating personality. In no case will it be found to be the cause of the rest of the neurotic structure—the basic origin of neurosis—although after it is established, it may contribute to the problem.[165]

A similar comparative study conducted by Michael Shofield in England, *Sociological Aspects of Homosexuality*, supports Hooker's observations.

The Trustees of the American Psychiatric Association, in their meeting of 15 December 1974, by a unanimous vote ruled that "homosexuality" shall no longer be listed as a "mental disorder" in its official nomenclature of mental disorders. Formerly the Association's list of mental disorders included it as a "sexual deviation." The category of homosexuality is now replaced by "sexual orientation disturbance," which is described as follows:

> This category is for individuals whose sexual interests are directed primarily toward people of the same sex and who are either disturbed by, in conflict with, or wish to change their sexual orientation. This diagnostic category is distinguished from homosexuality, which by itself does not necessarily constitute a psychiatric disorder. Homosexuality per se is one form of sexual behavior and, like other forms of sexual behavior which are not of themselves psychiatric disorders, is not listed in this nomenclature of mental disorder.

Kimball-Jones concludes from his survey of opinions concerning the psychological nature of homosexuality that "there is far too little evidence available at the present time to decide one way or the other whether or not homosexuality is inherently a psychiatric abnormality."[166] This conclusion is important, as we shall see, from the moral viewpoint, since it precludes any universal condemnation of homosexual practices as morally wrong based on so-called "reliable scientific evidence" that they are necessarily universally destructive of personality.

John Milhaven, for example, attempts to argue on the basis of psychological evidence that homosexuality is a mental disease, that all homosexual relations are necessarily destructive of both parties and, therefore, ultimately immoral. Milhaven agrees that the Christian who lives by the new morality bases all his moral judgment and his life on "something positive though general: the absolute divine command to *love*.

> Facing the question of homosexual behavior they would say: "God has laid down no specific and absolute prohibition of homosexual behavior. But He and I want absolutely one thing: that I live a life of love."[167]

Love is not just a question of feeling; experience teaches the honest man that some of his affectionate impulses lead to actions which in the long run hurt very badly the person he loves. Love, then, must be understood as "the free determination, commitment of a man or woman to further the good of a certain person." Milhaven admits that this is an old principle; its newness has to do with an *exclusive* reliance on experience rather than on a priori laws. However, since any one man's experience of homosexuality is extremely limited, we must turn to the experience of the community; we must turn "to those who have extensive critical experience, preeminently the psychologists, psychiatrists and analysts." As a consequence, Milhaven makes use of the testimony of members of that group of psychiatrists and psychologists who, as we have seen earlier, hold the extreme position that homosexuality represents universally an "arrest of personality growth, stunted development, disturbed personality." Although he grants that these conclusions are not scientifically certain and other psychiatrists and psychologists dissent, nevertheless Milhaven sees this conclusion as the "most reliable experience in our community at the present time." He draws the following conclusion from this evidence:

> A man having genuine love for himself and others will refrain, in his behavior, from expressing and deepening particular feelings when the evidence on hand indicates strongly, if not with absolute certainty, that the feelings are profoundly immature and disordered. Consequently a Christian moving in the spirit of the new morality condemns homosexual behavior more severely than one using traditional arguments. . . . According to the Christian, moved only by love, relying on the experience of the community, homosexual behavior is wrong in that it frustrates *the man himself*. It fixates him at a stage far short of the full emotional and sexual development of the "being man" who is God's glory.[168]

It is obvious that there is a great need for further research

and study in this area. But it is equally obvious that there is
no communal experience or prevalent psychological evidence
to justify Milhaven's conclusion. Since the available scientific
evidence leads to no necessary and universal conclusion, nor
even to a high degree of certainty, there is room left here for
a cautious discernment in each individual case as to the effect
a homosexual relationship is actually having on the personali-
ties of the individuals involved.[169]

The Controversy among Psychiatrists

A few words of critique from a moral viewpoint should be
written about the so-called scientific data derived primarily
from one school of psychiatrists and psychologists that is frequently invoked by moralists to buttress their condemnation
of homosexuality. As we have seen, these men define homosexuality a priori as abnormality. Accepting the Freudian
dogma that the sexual drive is the total economic content of
the human psyche, heterosexual development is defined as the
normal mature stage of development of the psyche. Moralists
should note that such a dogma represents a pansexualism
which precludes any recognition of a truly interpersonal dimension to human relations that in any way transcends the
purely instinctive sexual drive. Such a dogma, since it divorces
sexuality from its interpersonal context, deprives the moralist
of any right to convert purely psychiatric data based on this
dogma into moral judgment.

Further, psychiatrists deal exclusively with that portion of
the homosexual community who consider themselves psychologically ill and, as a result, seek psychiatric help. They seldom, if ever, come into contact with those homosexuals who
are living happy and fulfilled lives and who, since they do not
consider themselves ill, never seek the aid of a psychiatrist.
The frequently heard comment "I've never met a happy homo-

sexual" says more, perhaps, about the speaker than it does about the homosexual community.

Many psychiatrists manifest a very unscientific zeal in their effort to "cure" homosexuals. The relation between a willingness to change and success in therapy has led some clinicians to advocate what from a Christian point of view is a morally reprehensible procedure. Bergler, for example, speaks of "mobilizing any latent feelings of guilt."[170] What he seems to be advocating is a deliberate effort to increase the guilt feelings and self-hatred of the patient. Bieber, who goes along with this type of practice, reports only twenty-seven percent of his patients were cured under optimum conditions.[171] One wonders what happened to the other seventy-three percent who left therapy unconverted but burdened with false guilt and shame concerning their incurable condition. To continue to hold out the false hope of a "cure," in the light of almost total failure to truly effect a cure, is morally reprehensible; for nothing can be more destructive psychologically than to hold out a false hope to an already disturbed person. Connected with the issue of false hope is the danger of false guilt in the case where analysis fails to change sexual orientation. The great stress some clinicians place on the a priori condition, on the patient's part, of a will-to-change as a necessary factor for the success of therapy could lead many into further depths of self-accusation and despair. For if therapy should fail, as it usually does, patients could easily draw the false conclusion that failure was due to a fault of their will, for which they are morally responsible.

Notice should be taken here of another form of therapy which has recently received some publicity in the popular press, namely, behavior therapy based on a stimulus-response version of learning theory. The experiments reported consisted of, in one case, "injecting an emetic mixture subcutaneously" and showing the patient pictures of nude males while he is feeling distress, then administering testosterone while showing pictures of nude females.[172] Still another form used electrical shock in the same context. There is a serious moral problem concerning this therapeutic method, reminiscent of the type of medical experiment carried on in Nazi concentration camps. The effort involved here of trying to bypass normal human consciousness and free response in order to change patterns of response and consequent behavior could easily result in a deterioration of the entire human personality and undermine any future possibility of personal growth in the basic human factors of freedom and responsibility. Although one may end up with someone capable of copulating with the opposite sex, that action would, perhaps, no longer be a human action expressive of love.[173]

Fortunately, there seems to be a growing awareness in the scientific community of the false scientific pretensions as well as the anti-human and immoral attitude of some psychologists and psychiatrists. Thomas Szasz, for example, in his work *The Manufacture of Madness*, writes about the "great ideological conversion from theology to science," which redefined sin as sickness and moral sanction as medical treatment. "This change from a religious and moral to a social and medical conceptualization and control of personal conduct affects the entire discipline of psychiatry and allied fields. Perhaps nowhere is the transformation more evident than in the modern perspective on so-called sexual deviations, and especially on homosexuality."[174] Szasz accuses his fellow psychiatrists of involving themselves in a program of social control that has nothing to do with genuine scientific medicine. They arrive at this position by pretending that social conventions are identical with nature, and by confusing the question of disobeying a traditional personal prohibition with mental illness. "They establish themselves as agents of social control and at the same time

disguise their primitive interventions in the semantics and
social trappings of medical practice."[175] Clearly, Szasz maintains, the question the psychiatrist is posing when he speaks of
homosexuality as illness concerns not the traditional concept of
illness, but what moral or social significance contemporary
culture attaches to the homosexual's behavior.

> Psychiatry's preoccupation with the disease concept of homo-
> sexuality conceals the fact that the homosexuals are a group of
> medically stigmatized and socially persecuted individuals. The
> noises generated by their persecution and their anguished cries
> of protest are drowned out by the rhetoric of therapy. It is heart-
> less hypocrisy to pretend that physicians, psychiatrists or "nor-
> mal" laymen for that matter, really care about the welfare of the
> mentally ill in general, or the homosexual in particular. If they
> did they would stop torturing him while claiming to help him.
> But this is just what reformers—whether theological or medical—
> refuse to do.[176]

Szasz sees the modern medicine man playing the same role
vis à vis the homosexual community that the Inquisition did
of old. He points out that for many decades the insinuation of
homosexuality about one's adversaries has been an accepted
strategy in American political life. However, if the psychiatrist
really believes that homosexuality is an illness like any other,
why does he not protest when it is used as a means of social
degradation and political disqualification?

Szasz's conclusion is that psychiatric opinion about homosexuality is not a scientific proposition but a medical prejudice.
In fact, Bieber carries that prejudice to the absurdity of classify-
ing bachelorhood itself as a form of mental illness: "Failure to
marry in either sex is the consequence of the fear of it. There
is increasing recognition that bachelorhood is symptomatic of
psychopathology."[177] One can only wonder what treatment
(i.e., punishment) he would prescribe for the celibate priest
or religious? Another psychiatrist, Robert Lindner, concludes

that the psychiatric opinion concerning the homosexual as mentally ill reveals "the same hostility for the invert and his way of life and the same abhorrence of him as a person that has been the tradition in Western society.

> That we now employ such terms as "sick" or "maladjusted" to the homosexual appears to me to make little difference so far as basic attitudes and feelings are concerned. As a matter of fact, I suggest that precisely these designations reveal the ugly truth of our actual animus toward homosexuals and the sham of modern social-sexual pretensions; for in the current lexicon such words reflect the nonconformism of their referents—and nonconformism is the major, perhaps the only, sin of our times.[178]

As Dr. George Weinberg suggests in his recent book *Society and the Healthy Homosexual,* there is a serious problem leading to considerable pathological consequences which should concern psychologists and psychiatrists; that problem is not homosexuality as such but homophobia.[179] The disease of homophobia consists in an attitude held by a majority of homosexuals themselves. "It is not surprising that the homosexuals themselves often suffer from the conventional attitudes of revulsion and anger toward things homosexual. In their case the problem is even more serious than elsewhere—the attitude is a condemnation of self."[180] Weinberg believes that the essential issue is not whether one is homosexual but how the person handles his homosexuality if he is. Consequently, a major task for therapists should be to determine why some people regarded as deviants remain tormented while others are able to go on and live successful lives.

Even if a person is a heterosexual, however, a homophobic prejudice is certain to be harmful to him also. For such a person deprives himself not only of homosexual experience, which he truly does not want, but of all else he connects with homosexuality. Weinberg observes that most men who loathe homosexuals have a deadly fear of abandonment to passivity. "The surrender of control signifies to them a loss of masculinity, and their demand for control produces narrowness."[181] Yet the ability to be passive is essential to all learning experience. Further, they also feel under tremendous pressure to be the aggressor in all fields of life, especially in sexual activity. What remains to be explored is how the homosexual community, by liberating the heterosexual community from its homophobia, can help to liberate all mankind to a fuller and more human life.

Despite the exaggerations of some therapists, granted that he has some positive understanding of the homosexual and is free from the crippling effects of his own homophobia, the therapist can be an indispensable help to the individual homosexual who comes to him. The person who merely fears he may be a homosexual, or is attracted to the homosexual community, should explore every avenue toward the achievement of heterosexual capacities and relationships. This advice should be given independent of what one's moral judgment may be concerning homosexual relationships. If there is any hope of heterosexual adjustment in terms of psychological counseling, that escape from the difficulties of homosexual life should be explored. We shall deal at greater length with the question of heterosexual adjustment later on. However, even when there is no hope of heterosexual adjustment, therapy can still be a great benefit to many genuine inverts. A good counseling relationship can help them to self-acceptance and, consequently, open up the possibility of healthy and positive human relationships.

Part 2

Part 7

Toward a Positive Approach of Moral Theology

The greater part of both moral and psychological thinking concerning homosexuality tends to be prejudiced at its source, because it begins with a questionable presupposition. That presupposition, frequently explicit, maintains that the heterosexual condition is somehow the very essence of the human and at the very center of the mature human personality. Among moral theologians we have seen this at work in the assumption that heterosexual orientation is identical with the divine image in man. We met the same presupposition in a new context operative in at least one school of psychologists, represented by Irving Bieber, who begins his book *Homosexuality: A Psychoanalytic Study* with the statement: "We assume that heterosexuality is the biologic norm, and that unless interfered with all individuals are heterosexual."

Such an assumption effectively blinds the investigator to any evidence that a homosexual relationship can be a truly constructive and mature expression of human love, inasmuch as it holds that by definition mature and moral sexual love is heterosexual. As a consequence, the only avenue of investigation open to anyone operating within this prejudicial viewpoint is to examine the etiology of homosexuality, searching out presumed causes of deviation from the biologic and/or moral norm in faulty parental relations or in some constitutional causal factor. Further, this presupposition leaves only one course of action open to society, i.e. to do everything in its power to prevent homosexuality or, failing in this, to suppress all homosexual expression and seek a cure for its victims. In other words, society must treat homosexuals as carriers of a social and psychological disease to be handled in an analogous fashion to any physical disease, especially if it is considered contagious.

The Teleological Perspective

One can begin to detect, however, the beginnings of a totally different and more hopeful orientation of thinking in recent literature. The fruitful question is not "from whence" the homosexual came, but where he is going—or, better, to what purpose does he exist? As Pierre-Claude Nappey places the question:

> However much we may relativize the notion of a sexual norm and however much we may personalize the ethical exigency on which it is based, we are still not shedding any light on the reputedly obscure question of *why* homosexuality exists. . . . The question is not whether a certain type of behavior is excusable owing to the particular circumstances of the individual concerned, but whether it is an integral part of the much vaster behavioral pattern of the collectivity and whether it contributes in some way to its proper functioning.[1]

The peculiar importance of this question lies in the fact, as we have seen, that human sexuality participates in the radical freedom of man. Whatever participates in human freedom can only be understood adequately in terms of ideal goal or purpose. Consequently, it is only by also posing the question *why*, for what purpose, that we can hope to arrive at an adequate understanding of the human phenomenon of homosexuality.

For only by finding the answer to the teleological question can we detect in what sense homosexuality could be part of the divine plan and what intrinsic role it has to play in human society. As Nappey observes:

> Homosexuality must be seen . . . as corresponding to a definite finality. My own feeling is that not only is it possible for homosexuality to be of equal value with heterosexuality in individual cases, but that it has overall significance and a special role to play in the general economy of human relations, a role that is probably irreplaceable.[2]

I believe no more urgent task faces the moral theologian than the difficult and complex undertaking of determining that finality. For on its discovery depends both the ability of the homosexual to accept himself or herself with true self-love and understanding and the ability of the heterosexual society to accept a homosexual minority, not just as objects of pity and tolerance at best, but as their equals capable of collaborating in the mutual task of building a more humane society.

The Positive Contribution of the Homosexual Community

What, then, is the collective role of the homosexual minority in human society? And under what circumstances can that potential contribution become a reality? We have, perhaps, a clue to what that role is if we consider for a moment the frequently dehumanizing and depersonalizing role that prevailing sexual-identity images play in our culture. Dr. Harry Gershman, dean of the American Institute of Psychoanalysis, summarizes the objectionable stereotypes as follows:

> Men in our society are supposed to be strong, tough, assertive, objective, courageous, logical, constructive, independent, unsentimental, unemotional, aggressive, competitive, diligent, disciplined, level-headed, controlled, practical, promiscuous and persuasive. Women, in turn, are supposed to be weak, passive, irrational, emotional, empty-headed, unassertive, subjective, il-

logical, dependent, fitful, devoted, self-effacing, impractical, artistic and receptive.[3]

Commenting on these stereotypes, Dr. Eleanor Yaknes observes that gender identity is "the result of programming. Aside from the different physiology and anatomy, and vive la différence, I cannot think of any characteristic that is uniquely the property of either sex."[4] However, God help the man who may display a quality which society presupposes belongs exclusively to women, or vice versa.

An even more serious consequence follows if we assume that these heterosexual identity images constitute the total mature content of the human personality. For this results in the tendency to understand the human individual as essentially partial and incomplete. No human person is seen as complete in himself or herself, but only as essentially dependent on the other for his or her completion. The insights derived from the women's liberation movement have rendered us all sensitive to the depersonalized and unequal status of women in our culture. And since man usually achieves his own identity in his relation to woman, he in turn also suffers a depersonalized and partialized self-image. Thus the consequence of identifying with the heterosexual identity images proffered by our society is that the only type of heterosexual relationship that remains possible is a type of master-slave relationship, wherein the male seeks to dominate and the female seeks to be dominated. It is precisely this understanding of direct personal relationships between the sexes as necessary and inescapable that led Hegel to despair of solving the problem of human unity on the personal level, and to seek that solution on the political level in the unifying concept of citizen. Marx turned to class identity to escape the same dilemma. There is no need to detail here how the inevitable frustration and dependence that results from these images leaves modern man open to all forms of exploitation, both economic and political. Once one grasps the limitations imposed by the prevailing images, it is hardly surprising that a certain percentage of individuals fail to be acculturated successfully.

True Christian love, even married love, can only exist between persons who see themselves as somehow total and equal. Christian love must be love out of fullness and not out of need. It is not only the complementariness of the other sex that attracts, as Nappey observes:

> It is also the fact that while I sense that complementarity I can at the same time sense that here is a being who is whole and entire in himself (or herself) and, although endowed differently than myself, worthy of standing beside me and entering my life as an equal.[5]

It should be obvious that the stereotypes mentioned above negate any possibility of such a personal relationship for any heterosexual who takes them seriously.

The homosexual community has, perhaps, a special role to play in liberating the heterosexual community to a fuller understanding of themselves as persons by being an organic challenge within society to the partial and dehumanizing aspects of these sexual-identity images. Psychoanalysts maintain that all humans are basically bisexual, and that the normal process of becoming heterosexual involves a homosexual stage in which the child learns to identify with the parent of the same sex. The homosexual stage in the development of human sexuality has a narcissistic function. It is precisely this element of narcissism to which many moralists turn to buttress their moral condemnation of homosexuality, interpreting it in moral terms of selfishness. J. Edgar Brun, for example, makes this statement: "We may not be able to regard true inversion as a willful betrayal of the ordained social order, but the driving force of narcissism which is inevitably present in it feeds a selfishness

which can always destroy the dignity of human nature."[6] Such
a moral judgment makes sense only on condition that one
makes the sexual content of interpersonal relationships their
total economic content. Homosexual love seen as an interpersonal relation can be just as selfless and other-centered as
heterosexual love; in fact, since it escapes the debilitating
effects of the heterosexual identity images, perhaps it has a
better chance to form the basis of a genuine interpersonal love.
As Eugene Kennedy observes:

> Is it really too horrendous to believe that a homosexual may, ac-
> cording to the modality of his sexual adjustment, be reaching
> successfully out of himself and toward another person in his
> sexual activity? Is it not possible that his effort to move out of
> himself and toward the other is the difficult-to-read sign of
> genuine growth on his part? In other words, homosexuality, even
> if it is not human expression at its full term, may be a forward
> movement for the lonely and isolated individual who breaks out
> of his narcissistic self-concern.[7]

The narcissistic function of the homosexual stage is viewed
by some psychologists as having a positive function in human
sexual development:

> Thanks to that function, every individual of whatever sex can
> learn to love himself sufficiently in order to reach the point where
> he will be led to take an interest in things other than himself.
> This normal and legitimate dose of narcissism, this quantum of
> homosexuality, is what makes it possible for one human to be at-
> tracted to another.[8]

Nappey sees here not only a question of individual psychology
but of global, collective psychology. He sees, as a consequence,
the homosexual community as playing the role of objectifying
a necessary stage in human development. If the day should
come when it became possible to suppress all homosexual tendencies, so that the homosexual could disappear from the face

of the earth, we would then face the danger of removing a creative catalyst for the progressive development of sexual relations toward a fuller and more human reality:

> If heterosexuals honestly wish to see the perfect integration of persons and of the sexes, if they honestly hope to see the establishment of the best possible conditions for the fulfillment of individuals and of society as a whole, they will have to try and accept their own homosexuality through the acceptance of those in whom homosexuality is explicit. . . . Why shouldn't everyone be delighted that homosexuals have been entrusted *de facto* with the task and mission of attending the flame, or rather the two original flames, which, if they were to go out, would no longer serve as catalyzers of heterosexuality, thereby bringing about the downfall of the entire system.[9]

Eugene Kennedy points to the same creative role of the homosexual in relationship to the heterosexual community when he writes:

> When men can face with less fear the complex of feelings and impulses that are part of each person's sexuality, they will be able to accept and integrate their experience into a less prejudiced and more creative self-identity. That is to say, when persons can be more friendly toward what really goes on inside them, they will feel less pressure to deny or distort their experience of themselves; the achievement of their masculine or feminine identity will be less the acceptance of a rigidly imposed social stereotype and more the attainment of a multi-dimensioned truth about themselves. Greater openness to self can only increase our chance of more successful gender identity.[10]

Homosexuality and the Relation of the Sexes

In this respect it is interesting to note Jung's appreciation of the positive aspects of the male homosexual condition:

> If we take the concept of homosexuality out of its narrow psychopathological setting and give it a wider connotation, we can see

that it has positive aspects as well. . . . This [homosexuality] gives him a great capacity for friendship, which often creates ties of astonishing tenderness between men, and may even rescue friendship between the sexes from its limbo of the impossible. He may have good taste and an aesthetic sense which are fostered by the presence of a feminine streak. Then, he may be supremely gifted as a teacher because of his almost feminine insight and tact. He is likely to have a feeling for history, and to be conservative in the best sense and cherish the values of the past. Often he is endowed with a wealth of religious feelings, which help him to bring the *ecclesia spiritualis* into reality, and a spiritual receptivity which makes him responsive to revelation.[11]

In the first positive aspect that Jung indicates, he gives us a hint of another function which the homosexual community can play in society at large, one closely allied to the function just treated. Traditionally the married relationship between male and female found its support and stability in social roles, customs, and laws which rendered relatively secondary the type of direct personal relationship between the parties involved. But all these social supports are fast fading away, with the result that, as we have already observed, the divorce rate in the United States was recently reported to be rapidly approaching the fifty-percent mark. It is necessary, then, that the human family should find its primary support in the possibility of genuine personal love uniting husband and wife. It is interesting to note that one priest, acting as a canon lawyer in a marriage tribunal, claims that over one-third of the divorce cases he handled were based in the fact that one or the other partner was homosexually inclined. For as we have pointed out, many homosexuals attempt to hide their condition by entering into marriage.

If the homosexual community were allowed to play its role in society with full acceptance, homosexuals would cease to play their present negative role of undermining the marriage relationship, into which they have been forced by their desire to escape detection. Instead, they could potentially be a help in leading society to a new and better understanding of inter-personal love between equals—rather than the role-playing of tradition—as the foundation of the marriage relationship. The source of this liberating function of the homosexual community can be found in Jung's observation that "this [homosexuality] gives him a great capacity for friendship, which often creates ties of astonishing tenderness between men, and may even rescue friendship between the sexes from its limbo of the impossible." As we have seen, one often hears the opinion that homosexuality represents an immature form of sexual develop-ment at a narcissistic stage, which prevents the individual from appreciating the difference of the opposite sex. However, if Jung is correct in his observation, frequently it is the male heterosexual who, being under the influence of present sexual-identity images, is preoccupied with the opposite sex as "sexual object" to be dominated. Since he sees the other only in the generic context of sex object, he cannot relate to the other as truly other—that is, as person. Whereas the homosexual, to the extent that he has been freed from the depersonalizing effect of these images, is perhaps more free to encounter the opposite sex as total in himself or herself and as equal—that is to say, as person. Consequently, the homosexual community is in a special position to contribute to the liberation of the human community from depersonalized sexual relationships, and thus open up a new possibility of true love and friendship between the sexes.

In a particularly prophetic passage Ranier Maria Rilke had this to say about the changing role of the woman:

> We are only just now beginning to look upon the relation of an individual person to a second individual objectively and without prejudice, and our attempts to live such associations have no

model before them. . . . The girl and the woman, in their new, their own unfolding, will but in passing be imitators of masculine ways, good and bad, and repeaters of masculine professions. After the uncertainty of such transitions it will become apparent that women were only going through the profusion and the vicissitudes of those (often ridiculous) disguises in order to cleanse their own characteristic nature of the distorting influence of the other sex. . . . This humanity of woman, borne its full time in suffering and humiliation, will come to light when she will have stripped off the conventions of mere femininity in the mutations of her outward status . . . some day there will be girls and women whose name will no longer signify merely an opposite of the masculine, but something in itself, something that makes one think, not of any complement or limit, but only of life and existence; the feminine human being. . . . This advance will . . . change the love experience, which is now full of error, will alter it from the ground up, reshape it into a relation that is meant to be of one human being to another, no longer of man to woman. And this more human love (that will fulfill itself, infinitely considerate, and gentle, and kind and clear in binding and releasing) will resemble that which we are preparing with struggle and toil, the love that consists in this, that two solitudes protect and border and salute each other.[12]

It is the presence of the homosexual element in each individual which will help make such an accomplishment possible; and it is the collective presence of the homosexual community which will help provide the stimulus for such a development.

Homosexuality and Violence

Jung's brief development of the positive aspects of homosexuality indicates still another—and, perhaps, even more important—function that the homosexual community could perform within society toward the liberation of all to a more humane existence. Psychologists are fully aware of the deep all-pervasive relation between the male cultural identity image and the proneness to violence in the human community. As Dr. Weinberg observed, it is homophobia which frequently underlies the male aggressiveness and fear of passivity. The male image places an enormous stress on such elements as aggressivity and domination, qualities which are concretized in the folk heroes of male society—the soldier, the prizefighter, the football player, etc. The traditional need for the male member of society to be ready courageously to undertake violence in defense of his community explains the historical origins of the emphasis on these qualities. However, the social and cultural conditions which made these characteristics of the male necessary and desirable in the past have changed radically, and as a result they now pose a serious threat to the peace and progress of human society in general. Since the Koerner Report on violence in American culture we are well aware that the proneness to violence is a serious threat to our society. Unless we can find nonviolent means to resolve both national and international problems, humanity itself is seriously threatened. However, as long as the need of violence is built into our male-identity image there is little hope of finding such means. Every new generation will need its war for its young men to have the opportunity to prove their virility.

Those prophetic few who have chosen nonviolent means to try to correct injustices in our society have frequently been the victims of a popular hatred and antipathy which borders on the hysterical. Anyone who has participated in a peace demonstration or a civil-rights march knows from first-hand experience the type of emotional hostility their acts can provoke from the typical male onlooker. There is no doubt that many sense in the behavior of pacifists and conscientious objectors a menace to the male image itself.

Hitler's Nazi party was well aware of the association of pacifism with male homosexuality. In 1928 letters were sent to all German political parties asking for their position on reform of paragraph 175 of the German criminal code, a sodomy statute. The Nazi reply was as follows:

> Munich 14 May, 1928
>
> Community before Individual!
>
> It is not necessary that you and I live, but it is necessary that the German people live. And they can only live if they can fight, for life means fighting, and they can only fight if they maintain their masculinity. They can only maintain their masculinity if they exercise discipline, especially in matters of love. . . . Anyone who even thinks of homosexual love is our enemy. We reject anything that emasculates our people and makes them a plaything for our enemies, for we know that life is a fight, and it is madness to think that men will ever embrace fraternally. Natural history teaches us the opposite. Might makes right. And the stronger will always win over the weak. Let's see that we once again become the stronger.[13]

The homosexual community, once again granted that they were accepted and respected in the human community at large, have, perhaps, a very special and irreplaceable task to play in freeing the male community from this one-sided emphasis on violent characteristics. Because they may have fortuitously escaped the negative influence of the prevailing male identity image, they are potentially free from the psychological need to establish their male identity by means of violence. Jung's point is not that every homosexual presently realizes such a freedom—any more than every heterosexual necessarily succumbs to the depersonalization of heterosexual images. Occasionally homosexuals imitate in an exaggerated way the worst features of heterosexual images, for example the sadist-masochist style of relation. Violence seems on the whole remarkably absent among self-accepting homosexuals, while particularly prevalent among those who have strong homosexual desires they seek to repress. Norman Mailer's book *Why Are We in Vietnam?* "reveals a vision of America as cursed by the complex and hidden relationships between repression, dread of homosexuality and violence."[14] By liberating the heterosexual male to the possibility of recognizing and accepting the homosexual tendencies in himself a self-accepting homosexual community could make a positive and decisive contribution to bringing violence within control in society.

Homosexuality and Human Service

Another and connected change is occurring in modern society which also tends to place the person who is living out the traditional male image at a disadvantage. Traditionally the male had to be programmed to be the worker. Rendered insensitive to the needs of persons, he had to find his role in the hard work of dealing with material things. However, the cybernetic revolution has progressively eliminated the amount of hard work with material things necessary for the survival and prosperity of the community. In its place there is a growing demand for more and more people who are able to commit themselves to the types of service to their fellow humans which demand greater sensitivity and human concern. Traditionally, however, the service roles in the community—such as the care of the young and the aged, education, nursing, and social work in general—have been seen as primarily feminine roles, not fit occupations for the true male. As Jung observed, frequently the homosexual is "surprisingly gifted as a teacher because of his almost feminine insight and tact." Thielicke, in turn, speaks of the homosexual as frequently gifted with a remarkable "pedagogical eros, a heightened sense of empathy."[15]

Many observers note the attraction of homosexuals to artistic roles—actors, dancers, decorators, painters, etc. There is no doubt that the homosexual is freer to develop aesthetic values than is his male counterpart in the heterosexual world, and thus he has an important role to play in guiding humanity to a deeper appreciation of aesthetic values. However, what has remained relatively unnoticed is the attraction of many homosexuals to service roles, where they have been particularly successful. Many homosexuals find particular satisfaction in such positions as teachers, social workers, hospital orderlies, student counselors, psychologists, clergymen—in fact, in any form of occupation where they can be of direct service to their fellow humans. Three of the most gifted homosexuals for whom it has been my privilege to act as counselor were all extraordinarily successful in their work with retarded children. How often, too, have elderly sick parents been supported and cared for selflessly by a bachelor son or daughter whose homosexuality was carefully hidden from them; whereas, if they had been left to the mercy of their married, heterosexual offspring, they would have been committed to the impersonal care of some institution. Once again, there is the hopeful possibility that the homosexual community could serve the human community as a whole by making the male free to do works of service in the human community without feeling guilty about betraying the standards of his male identity.

Another positive effect that homosexuality can have on the individual, according to Jung, is his "feeling for history" and his resultant tendency "to be conservative in the best sense and cherish the values of the past." Since the majority of the traditional values have their basis in the family structure as such, at first glance this observation of Jung's seems rather paradoxical: for the homosexual appears to many as a threat to the family structure and, as a consequence, a threat to all the values traditionally associated with it. However, most of these traditional values represent customs, mores, and taboos imposed from without to which the majority grant uncritical conformity. Forced because of his condition to live for the most part outside these structures, the self-accepting homosexual is thrown back on himself and his own experience in order to reestablish the values which merit his acceptance.

Almost in direct proportion to the extent that he is cut off from traditional patterns, he must seek out and re-create the real values which these patterns were meant to convey and preserve them by his personal commitment.

Once again, the cultural male-identity image carries with it the frontier spirit of deserting the old in order to construct the new *ab ovo;* whereas the female image carries with it the task of preserving continuity and bringing the best of the old into the new. The homosexual, by escaping the confines of the male image, is relatively free to develop a sensitivity to the true values of the past, and his isolation from normal structures forces him to attempt new incarnations of these values.

The Role of the Lesbian

Unfortunately Jung's comments were limited for the most part to the positive role of the male homosexual. Let us consider for a moment the specific contribution of the lesbian. Just as the heterosexual male is expected to suppress many human qualities in order to conform to a narrow cultural identity image, even more so the heterosexual female must suppress many essential human qualities—qualities such as spontaneity, aggressiveness, intelligence, initiative, etc.—in order to conform to the narrow cultural identity image of a woman. On occasion the lesbian, by being able to escape the heterosexual cultural identity image, is freer to develop her total personality. In his article "Far from Illness: Homosexuals May Be Healthier than Straights," Dr. Mark Freedman concluded from a series of tests administered to both male homosexuals and to lesbians that "a clear picture of homosexuals today would show a great many men and women who live by their own values and whose emotional expressions aren't limited by traditional sex roles." Many gay people respond to social pressure against homosexuality with an intense quest for identity, purpose, and meaning. Dr. Freedman found the homosexuals he tested superior to their heterosexual counterparts in such psychological qualities as autonomy, spontaneity, orientation toward the present, and increased sensitivity to the value of the person.[16]

Many lesbians feel that they are persecuted by society primarily not because they are lesbians but because they are women. Whereas just the opposite is true for male homosexuals; they are persecuted because they are homosexuals, and not because they are male. Consequently, many lesbians believe that the primary liberation movement to which lesbians should be committed at this point in history is women's liberation, and only secondarily to gay liberation. As we have seen, G. Rattrey Taylor, in his book *Sex in History*, finds a universal phenomenon in patriarchal cultures; these cultures always tend to combine a strongly subordinational view of women with a repression and horror of male homosexuality. Whereas cultures based on a matriarchal principle are inclined to combine an enhancement of the status of women with a relative tolerance for male homosexual practices.[17] Consequently, there is an intimate connection between gay liberation for men and women's liberation, so that any real advance in either cause necessarily will represent an advance in the other.

The Homosexual and the Church

These reflections bring us to Jung's final, surprising observation concerning the positive aspects of male homosexuality. This has to do with the particular gift the homosexual community has received which renders it capable of contributing in a special way to the spiritual development of humanity.

> He [the homosexual] is endowed with a wealth of religious feelings which help him to bring the *ecclesia spiritualis* into reality, and a spiritual receptivity which makes him responsive to revelation.[18]

The components of that particular gift have already been recognized. For we have already noted that the homosexual community enjoys a special freedom which potentially could allow it to escape a hyperactive, aggressive, closed attitude and allow it to be passive and receptive; attitudes which are essential to prayer and the reception of revelation. It is no accident that in those cultures where the "machismo" image reigns, religious prayer and worship are considered activities only fit for women. The homosexual can be free from a need of violence and dedicated to the quest of peace. He can have a special sensitivity to the value of the person, especially the persons of the opposite sex. He can dedicate himself to a life of service of his fellow humans. Further, we have seen that the homosexual community, if it were granted freedom to be itself and exercise its talents, could contribute to the liberation of all humanity to a fuller realization of personhood.

There is an ideal identity image of what it means to be a full human person proffered to us by God in the New Testament; that image is given us in the person of Jesus Christ. Each of the special qualities Jung attributes to the homosexual community is usually considered as a striking characteristic of Christ—the qualities which distinguished him from the ordinary man. Christ had an extraordinary ability to meet the individual as a unique person; where others saw a class, a type, a sexual inferior, Christ manifested the ability to encounter the person with understanding and love. He also frequently expressed the desire to free his disciples from stereotypes and cultural prejudices. Christ refused to establish his identity and accomplish his mission by means of violence, and called on his disciples to be men of peace, resisting injustice by their own suffering. Again, Christ presented himself as a loving servant of all humanity, pointing out to his disciples that the pagan seeks to dominate and to be served, but his disciples must seek not to be served but to serve.

The point I am trying to make here is, obviously, not that Christ was a homosexual—any more than he was a heterosexual in the usual significance that the cultural context gives that designation—but, rather, that he was an extraordinarily full human person and an extraordinarily free human being. It is interesting to note that many successful celibate priests and religious, since they have escaped by means of their celibacy the negative effects of cultural identity images, have succeeded in incarnating these positive qualities of the Christ image in a striking way.

Paul makes the claim that there was a seed planted by Christ, the seed of the Spirit, whose eventual fruit will be the overcoming of all divisions that separate man from man, and thus separate each of us from the totality of ourselves (Gal. 3:28). He mentions three such divisions: master-slave (i.e. all divisions based on aggression and domination), Jew-Greek (i.e. all divisions based on racial or cultural difference), and finally the division between male and female. Obviously, Paul is not referring to an elimination of the biological and—if any—the psychological differences, but to the learned cultural distinction which renders women inferior to men, denies them the full status of persons, and thus prevents a true interpersonal love encounter between men and women. It is this same cultural distinction which, as we have seen, lies at the base of cultural homophobia and leads to the active persecution of the homosexual.

In Paul's mind, ideal human nature lies in the future, not in the past. It is up to the creative freedom of man with God's grace and the model presented in Christ to direct his development toward that ideal. That ideal is the fully mature human person. As we have suggested, the homosexual community, if it is allowed to be itself and develop its special qualities, has a very special role to play in bringing about that ideal both for its own members and for their heterosexual brothers and sisters—until we all "reach mature manhood, and that full measure of development found in Christ" (Eph. 4:13).

This summation of the potentially positive characteristics of the homosexual community runs the danger of creating another stereotype, albeit a positive one. Jung can be misread as portraying a romantic image of the homosexual which suggests that somehow he is better than his heterosexual brother or sister. Perhaps the greatest source of prejudice in the past has been the existence of certain negative stereotypes in the popular imagination. The male homosexual was assumed to be effeminate, artistically inclined, cowardly, unfaithful, promiscuous, a hater of women, a child-molester, an active perverter of youth, etc. No more important fact needs to be established than the fact that the homosexual is usually no less varied than his heterosexual counterpart, for the most part no better and no worse. There are violent homosexuals as well as nonviolent; there are artistically sensitive and insensitive, there are relatively selfish and unselfish, religiously sensitive and insensitive, morally committed and uncommitted, weak and strong, sexually promiscuous and faithful. Consequently, I have no desire to create a new stereotype, albeit a positive one.

The true fact is that there is no such being as a homosexual, any more than there is such a being as a heterosexual: there are human beings who happen to be, relatively, heterosexually or homosexually inclined. And these persons are as varied in their qualities and sensitivities as is humanly possible. Consequently, to assume that any general characteristic, whether negative or positive, necessarily applies in each particular case leads to a falsification of reality. Rather, we must be prepared to meet each individual person, whether heterosexually or homosexually inclined, on his or her own merits without the falsification of the encounter that comes from stereotypes. Charles Curran, in a recent article, remarks that "homosexuality can never be an ideal." I agree completely. But then, heterosexuality as such can never be an ideal either. The only ideals involved in all questions of sexual orientation are the great transcendent questions of justice and love.

The essential point I have tried to establish in stressing the positive characteristics of homosexuality is that the tendency to identify oneself as a person with one's sexual-identity image can, and frequently does, lead to a one-sided stress on certain qualities and the elimination of others. The heterosexual tends to define himself in contrast to the homosexual; the homosexual, in turn, tends to define himself in contrast to the heterosexual. The result is a narrow, impoverished, and dehumanizing self-image for both parties. The objective acceptance of the homosexual community will potentially leave both communities free from the need to conform to narrow stereotypes, and positively free to develop all the qualities that belong to the fullness of the human personality.

Part 3

VII

Pastoral Ministry to the Homosexual Community

The Failure of Pastoral Ministry

One final problem from the viewpoint of moral theology remains to be explored; that is the necessary changes in the nature of the Church's ministry to the homosexual community, granting the change in the nature of the Church's moral judgment on homosexual relationships which we have argued for. Paul Lehmann, as we have seen, made the point that the concern of Christian ethics should be to relate the intimate reality of sex in all its forms, including homosexuality, to the freedom and integrity of human wholeness. Consequently, Christian sexual ethics should accent the fundamental importance of the sexual act for the humanization of man and the setting in which that humanization of man is a concrete and achievable reality.[1] How, then, from the Church's viewpoint can it provide the spiritual setting within which the homosexual community can achieve its fullest moral and spiritual development?

There is no question that in the past the Church has made no attempt in this direction. It will be recalled that in its resolution on ministry to the homosexual community in Denver in 1972, the National Federation of Priests' Councils reported that "the Church's concern for and ministry to the homosexual community is practically invisible and therefore non-existent in the United States." Consequently, the Federation voted to establish "a task force to develop a model for a Christian ministry to the homosexual community."[2]

The nonexistence of such a ministry in the past is easily understood. Since it regarded the homosexual condition and all homosexual relationships at best as necessarily "objectively sinful" and somehow contrary to the divine will, the Church logically has refused to grant any recognition to homosexual relationships and, thus, to the homosexual community as such. Individual priest-counselors and confessors have manifested genuine compassion and pastoral concern for the individual penitent. It should be remarked, however, that the priest, like the psychiatrist, tended to encounter only those homosexuals who have internalized the judgment of the Church and of society, and hence experienced their condition as somehow sinful and productive of guilt and self-contempt. And frequently, since the priest has himself shared society's homophobia, even that minimal human compassion for the penitent has been lacking. A few years ago a report by a Lutheran pastor on a West Coast conference on homosexuality carried the following headlines in a Catholic newspaper: "Homosexuals Ask Churches to Accept Them." In that report one of the homosexuals interviewed at the conference had this to say:

> The Church is only for the majority and is always measuring up to conformity. I have no place to go, and it's impossible to become an atheist. First of all, every guy has got to have some place to go, even if he is not a devout and saintly person. Going to Church and confession sort of makes a person feel that he isn't alone. After all, a bed partner is only for a couple of minutes, hours or for a whole night—but God lasts forever. If the Church would only recognize that we are all members of the flock. They

don't have to bless homosexuality or say it's fine, but just say: You are a little spotted, but you are children of the flock.

Not only the homosexual himself but many professional people who deal with homosexuals believe that very frequently the Church tends to reject the homosexual. In the introduction to his book *Toward a Christian Understanding of the Homosexual,* H. Kimball-Jones, a Methodist minister and counselor whom we have quoted earlier, has this to say:

> There are untold thousands of homosexuals in America today who are forced to live secret lives, forced to live in constant doubt and fear, lest they be discovered and labeled as outcasts of society. . . . Their sexual anomaly has made them potential criminals in the eyes of the law and sinners in the eyes of the Church. The Church for the most part has made no attempt to understand them; along with the rest of society, it has viewed them with great contempt, closing its doors to them, failing to recognize them as children of God.[3]

In their book *Counseling the Catholic,* Robert Gleason and George Hagmaier make the point that many homosexuals feel abandoned by the Church because of inept pastoral counseling:

> The tragic reception which many a homosexual has received from a well-meaning but ineffectual or sometimes even hostile priest at least partially explains how so many of these unfortunates leave the Church in frustrated rebellion or deep despair . . . it is easy for him to conclude that the Church has abandoned him too.[4]

Gordon Westwood, in his work *A Minority: A Report on the Life of the Male Homosexual in Great Britain,* noted that 61 percent of his homosexual contacts had turned at one time to the Church for help, but only 6 percent said that they obtained help with their homosexual problem from their religion; while 5 percent more stated that their religious belief had offered them some comfort. However, 81 percent reported no help or comfort from religion.[5] As John Cavanagh pointed out in a lecture at Catholic University:

> Many counselors look upon the homosexual with mixed feelings. They have been known to be fearful, mistrusting, resentful, and sometimes overcome by feelings of inadequacy. Many have frightened the deviate away with their rudeness and hostility. They may associate all homosexuality with willful depravity, seduction of the young, effeminacy, and moral perversion. . . . Because of these attitudes many homosexuals do not seek advice, which may lead some counselors to think that homosexuality is a rare thing. I have been told by priests of over twenty years experience that they have never seen a homosexual.[6]

Personal Ministry to the Individual

Most experts are in agreement that a clergyman, granted that he has minimal knowledge of the psychological aspects of the problem of homosexuality and is free from popular prejudices and misconceptions, can be of important and even essential help to the homosexual, and especially to a member of his Church who has this problem and seeks his assistance. More frequently than not, the person with a homosexual problem has introjected the attitude of society toward himself. He suffers great mental anguish and a profound sense of alienation, often believing himself to be an outcast not only from human society but from divine love as well. No person with heterosexual tendencies would be inclined to answer the question: Who are you? with the response: I am a heterosexual. But if he felt free to do so, this would be the response of the homosexual. Whether he carefully conceals his homosexual condition or expresses it openly, the person with a homosexual orientation tends to accept his homosexuality as his deepest self-identity image, the most important single fact about himself. And because he tends to accept his image from the attitudes of the people about him, the person who believes himself to be a homosexual frequently has a negative self-image which leads to self-hatred and self-destruction.

Homosexuals will never be able to master their sexual drive in a positive way and integrate it successfully into their whole personality development until they become aware of themselves as persons of infinite dignity and worth, worthy of their fellow human's respect and consideration. In order to eliminate this self-destructive image and arrive at a positive self-identity image of themselves as persons of value, it is absolutely necessary that persons who have a homosexual orientation find someone with whom they can be completely open and still be treated with respect and love. What militates against such a self-disclosure, however, is the frequent conviction that no one will continue to respect them as persons if they reveal the true nature of their problem.

Logically, by his calling and his profession the clergyman should be the person to whom the homosexual could turn with complete confidence. And very often—some authors estimate at least forty percent of the time—the clergyman is the first person to whom he turns and reveals his problem. If, however, the homosexual should fail to receive a sympathetic reception, which unfortunately often seems to be the case, he could easily lose all hope. On the other hand, the very fact of being able to speak openly about his problem for the first time with a respected member of the community, who continues to manifest respect for him, can be an essential step toward establishing hope, where previously there was only despair.

Even when the rare clergyman who understands the homosexual and has the courage to offer his ministry can be found, the very fact that he does such counseling can effectively ruin his career and destroy his reputation as a clergyman. The National Federation of Priests' Councils notes that "individual priests and ministers, working with homosexuals, usually encounter a social and psychological stigma as a result of their work, and this stigma is the single most effective obstacle to ministers who want to work with homosexuals."

The Church and the Reform of Civil Law

There is no question that frequently the homosexual in the United States today is the victim of great social injustice. He is frequently denied the fundamental human rights to association, work, housing, etc. The first step toward eliminating these injustices is a reform of law. We have seen how a legal tradition of suppression of homosexual practices sprang up in the Christian West as a result of a misunderstanding of the Sodom and Gomorrah narrative. In a recent hearing concerning the reform of legal discrimination against homosexuals in employment and housing in New York City, one politician found it necessary to oppose the bill because it would be contrary to "our Judaic-Christian heritage." He attempted to establish this point by referring to the Sodom and Gomorrah tradition. The Church obviously has a serious obligation to correct such a misunderstanding of authentic Christian tradition in the minds of the public.

Practically all the authorities consulted are in agreement that there is an urgent need from a legal viewpoint for reform of the present laws in the United States concerning homosexuality. Such reforms have been operative in most European countries since the Napoleonic Code, without any evident harm to the common good. Great Britain recently adopted these reforms as a result of the Wolfenden Commission Report. In all but three states in the United States homosexual acts between consenting adults are legally a criminal act, penalized in some states with long prison terms.

At the time of the Wolfenden Report debate in England, the Catholic Archbishop of Westminster acknowledged two "questions of fact" which, he believed, should determine the question of law reform. "Catholics," he commented, "are free to make up their minds on these two questions of fact." The two questions were:

1. If the law takes cognizance of private acts of homosexuals and makes them crimes, do worse evils follow for the common good?
2. Would change in the law harm the common good by seeming to condone homosexual conduct?

All authorities seem to agree in answering "yes" to the first question. There is little doubt that the present repressive laws against homosexuals quite unjustly penalize a minority group and cause unnecessary and untold pain, fear, and suffering to many people who are otherwise law-abiding and responsible citizens. Apart from the fearful toll of suffering, lost talent, and mental breakdown, etc., the present laws considerably increase criminal activity by the opportunity they offer for blackmail, entrapment, and other forms of intimidation. A recent trial in New York uncovered a blackmail ring that had earned millions of dollars in this manner.

The type of abuse these laws lead to on the political level is notorious. The fortunately unsuccessful attempt on the part of one of our major car manufacturers to silence a prominent critic, because he happened to be a bachelor, and therefore suspect, is a good example. Further, by giving the homosexual community the character of an outlawed minority these laws encourage a type of aggression based in homophobia. On many occasions the illegal status of the homosexual has combined with an emotional climate to give rise to hostility approaching psychotic proportions and violence that is unequivocally criminal. Once exposed or even suspected, the "homosexual" may become prey to the worst forms of cruelty and injustice at the hands of those who regard their cruelty as righteousness. On numerous occasions individuals or groups of men have established themselves "vigilantes" and have undertaken the practice of "queer baiting." One example, an instance which ended in tragedy for all concerned, occurred a few years ago in San Francisco. A group of young men (two of them from a private Catholic school) attacked, robbed, and assaulted a young school teacher they judged to be "queer." They left him unconscious on the street, where he was killed by an oncoming trolley—while the vigilantes continued their prowl of the city, looking for other victims. The inspector assigned to the case reported: "They said they considered Hall's death a justifiable homicide. They seem to regard the beating of whoever they consider deviants as a civic duty."

The moral question here concerns the source of the impression these young men had that assault and battery, robbery, and even murder are justified if the object of one's hostility is homosexual, or even only suspected to be so. Certainly even the clergyman who feels most strongly about the evils of homosexual practices has a duty in conscience to refrain from any words or actions which would help create the atmosphere in which such events become likely, or from seeming to give his tacit approval.

The American Law Institute in its model penal code recommended as far back as 1955 that private homosexual acts between consenting adults should be excluded from the criminal law because

> no harm to the secular interest of the community is involved, and there is a fundamental question of the protection to which every individual is entitled against State interference in his personal affairs when he is not hurting others.

The second question of fact the Archbishop asks is much more difficult to answer. It is, perhaps, true that many people believe what is legal is moral and what is immoral should be illegal. This popular confusion between legality and morality is the most serious obstacle to law reform. We have seen this confusion at work in the minds of many, for example, in the question of the reform of laws concerning abortion. The experience in the past with prohibition and in other fields has led the public to some realization that "one should not try to legislate morality." The emphasis in the Catholic Church since Vatican II on the right and responsibility of the individual to come to an independent moral judgment has also helped pave the way.

However, Christian educators and clergy cannot be content with merely registering a question of fact here. In the whole field of sexual morality there is a widespread confusion of morality with legality, to the serious detriment of the moral life. Most confessors and counselors are well aware how often the marriage license, for example, is understood as a license for an immoral use and abuse of one's marriage partner. Consequently, a serious responsibility rests on the shoulders of all who are involved in helping to form the conscience of the public to provide instruction in the ability to distinguish and to relate the moral and legal orders with their respective ends and procedures. This would prepare the way for a reform of law as well as a more mature attitude toward personal moral responsibility.

Some traditional authors express alarm that any let-up of legal discipline might result in a marked increase in homosexual behavior. But first of all, such legal reforms will certainly not contribute to any increase in the homosexual condition. There is no evidence that the legal status of homosexuality in any way influences the number of those who share this condition. However, there is a good reason to believe that the healthier climate that would result from such a legal reform could reduce the social pressures and consequent emotional disorders for those who share this condition. Secondly, there is no evidence that homosexual practices have increased in those societies where no such legal penalties exist or where they have recently been reformed. All these considerations lead to the conclusion that the Church has a serious moral responsibility out of both justice and charity to work for the reform of laws concerning homosexuals and do everything in its power to educate the faithful to the need of such a reform.

The Goal of Heterosexual Adjustment

Once he has established a positive relationship of understanding and respect, the clergyman-counselor's difficult task has just begun. If the clergyman is to offer the homosexual anything more than the essential step of acceptance in Christ, he must have some understanding of the nature of the individual's problem. Practically all authorities agree that the first goal of counseling should be to guide the person with a homosexual problem to a heterosexual adjustment whenever possible.

The person who merely fears he may be a homosexual, or is attracted to the homosexual community, should explore every avenue toward the achievement of normal heterosexual capacities and relationships. This direction should be taken independent of what one's moral judgment may be concerning homosexual practices. Even the officers of the Mattachine Society, a homophile organization, agree with this aim:

> On the basis of our experience—the embarrassment, shame and humiliation so many of us have known—we would definitely advise anyone who has not yet become an active homosexual, but has only misgivings about himself, to go the other way, if he can.

The reason for this advice is the many problems the average homosexual encounters, which make a positive adjustment to such a life extremely difficult. Among these difficulties can be enumerated: the typical homosexual's agonies of remorse and self-torture over what he feels to be his immoral desires,

whether these arise from conscious identity with the condem-.
nations of Church and society or from neurotic conflicts within
himself; his openness to blackmail and other forms of intimidation; his status of being outside the normal protection of
the law; his necessity continually to conceal what he frequently
believes to be his true identity from public view, with the
added threat that accidental revelation could result in loss of
his job, expulsion from school, dishonorable discharge from the
military service, loss of future security and job opportunities,
loss of friends and the respect of family and dependents. Still
other problems involve his propensity to sexual promiscuity
divorced from a complete and healthy interpersonal relationship; and the resulting tendency for sexual desires indulged
in, but never fully satisfied, to occupy a disproportionate place
in his life. Above all else, there is the very real threat of ultimate loneliness to one to whom all the normal structures of
society—marriage, children, dependents, etc.—are closed. It
should be noted, however, that all these negative aspects of
homosexuality are not necessarily due to homosexuality as
such, but are the results of both society's and the Church's
attitude to the homosexual.

All these rather common aspects of homosexual life can effectively paralyze all initiative, result in a feeling of inferiority,
and lead to an emotional breakdown which could make social
adjustment impossible. Therefore, if there is any hope of
heterosexual adjustment, that escape from the difficulties of
homosexual life should be explored.

So, the first discernment a counselor should attempt to establish is whether or not a given individual is a genuine homosexual or merely suffering from "pseudo-homosexual panic" as
a result of some experience of one of the many forms of conditional homosexuality. This discernment is especially important,
as Hettlinger notes, in dealing with the adolescent or young
adult. Quoting experts to the effect that "it is not until the age

of twenty-five has been reached or even later that we can be fairly sure that homosexual impulses are not just a phase of normal development," Hettlinger concludes:

> Even if on examination a student has markedly homosexual tendencies, no one within the normal student age range has reason to conclude that his homosexual urges, however strong, are either basic or permanent.[7]

D. J. West concurs in this judgment, stating: "When homosexual behavior represents a precarious solution to current conflicts or reflects the pressures of external circumstances, a change may well come about."[8] In such cases it is sometimes sufficient to point out the negative side of homosexual life and its obvious disadvantages in order to cure any illusions of homosexuality or any false images of a "gay" life. The author knows of one situation where a student-counselor was able to use the help of an older, well-adjusted homosexual to achieve this purpose with excellent results.

Whenever possible, of course, the clergyman-counselor is well advised to seek professional assistance in dealing with homosexuals. Where such assistance can be had, most authors agree that the clergyman himself should continue to see the individual and seek to offer supportive guidance in cooperation with the professional involved. In cases where the individual refuses such help, or for practical reasons such help is unavailable, the clergyman himself should continue his role as counselor and do the best he can. In this latter event, the clergyman should himself seek supervision in the management of his client.

Several moral problems face the counselor who accepts as his primary goal to lead the homosexual to a heterosexual adjustment. Among these is the problem of the danger of fostering false hopes of a cure in the mind of the homosexual. Despite the optimism of some psychiatrists concerning the possibilities of a cure, there is little real hope that a cure will be effected in the practical order for a large majority of the cases of true homosexuality. Even Bieber, one of the most optimistic psychiatrists, reports that only twenty-seven percent of his patients were cured under optimum conditions. As Cory and LeRoy remark in their book *The Homosexual and His Society:*

> Of those who came (or were sent) to Bieber and his co-workers for study, who struggled through analysis and underwent the torment and difficulties that it entails, many of them for literally hundreds of hours, more than 70 percent remained homosexuals. The writers are acquainted with hundreds of young men and women, and many older ones as well, who spent thousands of hard-earned dollars and hundreds of uncomfortable hours, seeking to overcome their imperious deviant drives, but in vain. The Mattachine Society and other groups have scores of members, some of whom readily admit that they were aided to face reality by the therapeutic sessions, but who were as overwhelmingly or as exclusively homosexual after therapy as they had been before.
>
> It would seem that 73 percent of failure is a large figure, and that this is the realistic statistic that should be publicized in order to obtain better self-understanding by the homosexual and better acceptance of him by society. To focus attention on the 27 percent, as if it were a sure-fire majority, is misleading and dangerous.[9]

As a consequence the counselor would be well advised to admit the limited chances of a therapeutic cure in more serious cases where the conditions are unfavorable. As William Lynch established in his book *Images of Hope,* nothing can be more destructive psychologically than to hold out a false hope to an already disturbed person. The counselor should also emphasize, however, that regardless of the question of heterosexual adaptation, therapy can still be of great benefit. Well over ninety percent of Bieber's patients reported "improvement which was not directly related to the sex problem." There is no doubt, then, that therapy can be very helpful to anyone suffering psychologically because of a homosexual problem, while in a limited number of cases it can result in a hetero-sexual adjustment. As we have seen, connected with the issue of false hope is the danger of false guilt, if analysis fails to change sexual orientation. As we have already pointed out, the great stress some clinicians place on the a priori condition on the part of the patient of a will to change as a necessary fac-tor for the success of analysis could lead many into further depths of self-accusation and despair. For if therapy should fail, they could easily draw the false conclusion that the failure of therapy was due to a failure of their will, for which they are morally responsible.

The Case For and the Case Against Sexual Abstinence

There is another factor that seriously hampers the ability of the Church to minister effectively to the homosexual. Granted the traditional moral judgment that homosexual relations are always necessarily sinful and contrary to the divine will, the only pastoral advice that could be given to the true homosex-ual, who could not change his sexual orientation, was to prac-tice sexual abstinence. In the words of Michael Buckley:

> The aim of all pastoral counseling of the homosexual should be ultimately his re-orientation to heterosexuality, and where this is impossible an adjustment to his condition in the only way accept-able to Catholic moral theology—a life of chastity.[10]

Cavanaugh agrees with Buckley, stating: "A clergyman should be content to set as his ultimate aim the adjustment of the homosexual to a life of chastity."[11] It is clear from the context of both authors that they understand by "chastity" uniquely a policy of total abstinence from all sexual expression. Neither author seems aware that there can be a chaste expression of sexuality insofar as it is a true expression of human love.

All moral considerations apart for the moment, there is no question that a life of abstinence from all sexual expression, if that life proves possible without serious damage to the person, remains a good prudential choice for the homosexual in today's society. The dangers and the difficulties of an active homosexual life are so great and the probability that, owing to guilt and self-hatred, a homosexual relationship may prove destructive both to the individual and to the other person involved is so high, that every Christian homosexual may be well advised to try to structure his life without an active sexual relationship. As a result, if there is any hope that a life of abstinence can be successfully undertaken, then it remains a reasonable choice. It should be noted once again, however, that all these negative aspects of homosexuality are not necessarily due to homosexuality as such but are the result of both society's and the Church's attitude to the homosexual.

The clergyman-counselor should show a sensitive awareness of what he in fact is demanding of a homosexual when he urges him to undertake such a life of abstinence. For example, Cavanaugh's statement: "Just as we expect the heterosexual to be continent outside of marriage, so, too, the homosexual"[12] demonstrates just such a lack of sensitivity to the homosexual's special dilemma. The heterosexual's abstinence is either a temporary condition or one he has freely chosen; whereas the abstinence the Church would impose on the homosexual is involuntary and unending. In attempting to live out a life of abstinence, the adult male homosexual will first of all have to avoid any close relationship with women. Such a friendship in our culture would almost certainly be understood as prelude to marriage. And if there is any advice one can almost certainly give in most cases, it is that the homosexual is morally obliged never to enter marriage while there is any reasonable doubt that he may be a true homosexual. In fact, canon lawyers are seriously debating the question whether or not such a marriage would be necessarily invalid, since a true homosexual would be incapable of a valid consent to the marriage bond. There are many instances reported where homosexuals have entered into marriage, concealing their condition from their partner, in order to disguise their condition and win social acceptance. The tragic results for all parties concerned need not be detailed.

Cut off from close relations with women because of his condition, the homosexual is traditionally exhorted to cut off any deep, personal relationships with men, because they would serve as "the occasion of sin." Cavanaugh advises the counselor to urge the homosexual to avoid all former homosexual companions; in forming new friendships, to avoid any individual who is "sexually attractive"; to live alone; to avoid work with boys; to avoid entry into the military service; not to enter the clergy or religious life, etc. Indeed, he carries this type of advice to its logical conclusions by advising that the homosexual should avoid any "romantic" friendships, even if chaste:

> One of the principles of conduct that an invert should formulate is that, because of his special condition, there is no value in allowing himself to form or to continue romantic friendships (i.e. those in which sexual attraction is a determining element) with people of his own sex, no matter how chaste the relation may be. Even if the invert is continent in these friendships, it is, nevertheless, a human love which can be never fully realized or satisfied licitly. It will, therefore, inevitably lead to anxiety and depression.[13]

In other words, in the pursuit of a life of "chastity" the homosexual should deny himself not only genital sexual relations, but every expression of warm human affection. Every psychologist worth his salt is well aware that all human affection and friendship is normally colored by a diffused, non-genital form of sexual attraction. Cut off, then, from all deep and affectionate female and male friendship, the homosexual is literally condemned to a living hell of isolation and loneliness. And such a life is not urged temporarily, but must be sustained until death, under threat of possible eternal damnation. As black novelist James Baldwin observes:

> The really horrible thing about present-day homosexuality . . . is that today's unlucky deviate can only save himself by the most tremendous exertion of all his forces from falling into an underworld in which he can never meet either man or woman, where it is impossible to have either a lover or a friend, where the possibility of genuine human involvement has altogether ceased. When this possibility has ceased, so has the possibility of growth.[14]

Cavanaugh somewhat tempers his advice, however, by quoting the following from Hagmaier and Gleason:

> The uninformed confessor has a tendency to demand that the invert avoid every contact which might possibly be a source of stimulation for him, e.g., swimming, sports, stag society, artistic circles, male friendships. In many cases such involvements help drain off a more basic urge for physical contact. To stifle these outlets could very well precipitate the penitent into more frequent and more overt homosexual activity.[15]

In line with this advice, frequently those writing from a traditional viewpoint advise the homosexual to sublimate his sexual urges by committing himself to an active and productive life. What they sometimes fail to realize is that they have eliminated a priori under the rubric of "avoiding the occasion of sin" those very activities for which the homosexual is very often best suited, and by means of which he would have some chance of achieving a wholesome sublimation. As Kimball-Jones observes:

> While he might stand the best chance of sublimating his sexual drives in professions such as scouting, teaching and the Christian ministry, professions which involve what Thielicke calls a "peda-

gogical eros . . . a heightened sense of empathy," it is difficult for a professed homosexual to enter into such professions.[16]

There is a growing body of evidence that for a majority of true homosexuals sublimation and a life of sexual abstinence is not a practical pastoral answer to their problem. Counselors sometimes seem to be unaware of, or forget, the fact that psychologists understand sublimation as an unconscious process, which, as a result, cannot be the direct object of one's will. As Gordon Westwood indicates, "Sublimation is an unconscious mechanism and can be a useful aid, but it is rarely a full controlling factor. Whereas forced abstinence from fear and guilt often leads to neurotic disorders."[17] Ellis and West both report sublimation relatively ineffective as a therapeutic goal.[18] Marcus Hirshfield found such therapy to be effective in less than five percent of the homosexuals with whom he attempted it.[19]

Unfortunately, since the role of permanent confessor or spiritual father has all but disappeared from the scene in the United States, most confessors do not have any sort of follow-up on the penitents they advise. But those clergyman-counselors who do stay with the persons they direct are well aware how frequently the true homosexual who attempts a life of abstinence will go a month, a year, even several years, only to end up indulging in promiscuous, often compulsive sex, calculated to lead to social ruin and psychological breakdown. In homosexual circles the person who leads a life of abstinence in his home town, only to fall victim to the worse forms of promiscuity with all its inherent dangers on his annual visit to the big city, is a notorious figure.

The insistence of the Church on total abstinence as the only morally feasible alternative for the genuine homosexual who cannot change his sexual orientation has led to the paradoxical result, even if unintentional, of promoting promiscuity and humanly destructive and depersonalized sexual activity among Catholic homosexuals. If a Catholic homosexual confessed occasional promiscuity, he could receive absolution and be allowed to receive communion in good conscience. If, however, he had entered into a genuine permanent love relationship, he would be judged in "a state of sin," and unless he expressed a willingness to break off that relationship he would be denied absolution. Consequently, the traditional discipline unwittingly tended to undermine the development of healthy interpersonal relationships among homosexuals and gave the appearance that the Church disapproved more of the love between homosexuals than it did of their sexual activity as such. One can see a parallel here with the similar paradoxical result of the Church's attitude on fornication and cohabitation. If a Catholic were involved in promiscuous heterosexual activity, he or she could receive absolution. However, individuals who entered into a permanent relationship outside of marriage, and thus attempted to establish a fuller human relationship, were judged to be in "a state of sin" and must be denied absolution and the right to receive holy communion.

Again we restate, if a person with homosexual tendencies with God's grace can successfully undertake a life of abstinence without destructive emotional conflicts and personality breakdown, then he or she is certainly well advised to do so. But what is troubling many counselors and confessors, as well as many moral theologians, is the realization that a majority of their clients or penitents who fall into the category of true homosexuals will in all probability not be successful in such an attempt, no matter how hard they pray or strive. On the contrary, the almost inevitable results will be tragic in terms of suffering, guilt, and mental disorder. The whole enterprise becomes all the more suspect with the dawning awareness that the moral judgment which makes such a pastoral practice necessary is not so much a true moral judgment as it is an expression of historical and cultural prejudice.

There are a number of other factors which are causing many to question the absolute validity of the Church's traditional pastoral stance in relation to the homosexual. Surely, the present crisis concerning a life of abstinence in the priesthood and religious life should give rise to some reconsideration. If priests and religious, who attempt a life of chastity under optimum conditions of both nature and grace, are finding difficulty in ever growing numbers, how can we demand such a life from the average homosexual, who shares none of the helps or motivations to be found in clerical or religious life?

One factor which probably influences the absolute nature of the traditional stand has to do with clerical values and mentality. In an interesting research study into the differences between typical clerical and lay value systems, priest-psychologist William Hague discovered that whereas the priest is inclined to rate "salvation" first in his scale of values, the layman is inclined to place "love" first and give "salvation" a relatively lower rating. Hague makes this observation:

> We find our identity in our relationships with others. One cannot base an identity on mere superficial "helping" relationships, no matter how dedicated or religious the motives may be. When a crisis comes, there isn't the personal human security there to withstand it. . . . Deep intimate human relationships are the ground in which personality takes roots and lasting security is found.[20]

Hague suggests that this insight helps explain the number of excellent men—still very much in love with their priesthood—who have chosen to leave it for a more personal relationship of marriage. In an analogous fashion, many a homosexual is faced with the dilemma of continuing his relationship with the Church at the price of his loss of any deep human relationship and the loss of his own growth and development in his personal self-identity, or of seeking his personal growth and identity by means of such a relationship only at the price of cutting himself off from the Church. Just as many priests are of the opinion that celibacy should not be a necessary condition of their priesthood, but open to voluntary choice, so many Catholic homosexuals believe that a life of sexual abstinence should not be required of them because of their condition, but open to voluntary choice.

The traditional exhortations that the homosexual can achieve sanctity by accepting the sufferings and difficulties which would result from the diminishment of his personal life and his psychological problems seem to be based frequently on a very questionable sort of dualism between human and spiritual development. They tend to negate the implications of insight attributed to Saint Irenaeus: "The glory of God is man fully alive." One recalls Saint Augustine's exhortation to one of the first communities of religious, in which he points out that "the foolish virgins without oil in their lamps" were indeed chaste, but their chastity was without love; they were incapable of a warm, loving response to the human needs of others, and thus were excluded from the kingdom of God, which is a kingdom of love. There can be a type of sexual abstinence which tends to be morally evil and psychologically destructive. There can be no necessary conflict between the human and spiritual fulfillment of man.[21]

What Kimball-Jones suggests is that if the Church is to be of any help to the majority of true homosexuals who cannot change or successfully lead a life of abstinence, then it must begin at the point where they find themselves. The question is not whether or not they are in a state of sin, but rather how they can make the best of a given, and in many cases, unchangeable situation. As Thielicke poses the question:

Perhaps the best way to formulate the ethical problem of the constitutional homosexual, who because of his vitality is not able

to practice abstinence, is to ask whether in the coordinated system of his constitution, he is willing to structure the man-man
relationship in an *ethically responsible* way. Thus the ethical
question meets him on the basis which he did not enter inten-
tionally, but which is where he actually finds himself. . . .[22]

Ministry to the Homosexual Community

These and many other factors have led the homosexual community in general and the Christian homosexual community
in particular to a new level of consciousness concerning its
needs and its rights in relation to the Church. Many Christian
homosexuals no longer accept the traditional judgment that
all homosexual relationships, precisely because they are homosexual, are necessarily sinful. Consequently, they are refusing
the pastoral aim of abstinence as a necessary goal and, in many
cases, as a desirable goal. As one group of Catholic homosexuals recently reported:

> The primary purpose of *Dignity* is to help the gay Catholic
> realize that to be Christian he need not deny his homosexuality,
> but rather he *should* be fully himself in order to be fully
> Christian. Dignity will fight for the right of the gay to use sex
> his own way. We have no intention of side-stepping the issue, or
> playing it down, or steering our members toward a celibate life.
> We do not want people merely to accept us as human beings. We
> want them to accept the fact that because we are human we
> have the right to use sex in the only way that is natural for us.
> When that is accepted, we will be seen very easily as morally
> and physically healthy, patriotic human beings.[23]

Further, important as individual counseling has been and
remains, it is no longer possible for the Church to perceive its
ministry to the homosexual as a ministry to individuals as
such; rather, it must begin to recognize that the only effective
ministry will be a ministry to the homosexual community. The
Christian homosexual has an imperative need of a social and

religious setting in which he can begin the long task of repair-
ing the wounds inflicted on his psyche by the prejudices of
society and the Church, as well as the positive task of attempting to integrate moral and religious values into his life-style as
a self-accepting homosexual. From their sociological study of
male homosexuality in three countries—the United States, the
Netherlands, and Denmark—Weinberg and Williams concluded: "Probably our most salient finding pertains to the bene-
ficial effects (in terms of psychological adjustment) of a supportive environment—social relations with other homosexuals,
their own institutions and publications."[24]

The Christian homosexual is well aware that such a religious
community can be truly helpful to him only if it is willing to
accept him as a homosexual and accept ethically responsible
homosexual relationships. The failure of the mainline Churches
to provide the homosexual with such a community has led to
the recent establishment of the "gay" Churches, such as the
Metropolitan Community Church. These homophile Churches
conceive of themselves as interim communities, necessary as
long as the heterosexual Church communities are incapable
of receiving, or unwilling to receive, the homosexual while respecting his life-style. The Metropolitan Community Church,
for example, claims that it is "working toward the day when
it can close its doors because the other Christian communities
with love and understanding will have opened theirs to the
gay people.

> Since the founding of the Church, it has occasionally been neces-
> sary for someone to step outside the regular Christian camp in
> order to point out its laxity in adhering to the loving spirit of
> its founder. . . . Each of these moments of re-evaluation of the
> Church's mission resulted in advances in mankind's eternal strug-
> gle to establish an environment in which every person has the
> opportunity to fully realize and develop his potential as a human
> being and a child of God. Metropolitan Community Church is

following this great tradition of endeavoring to be God's special instrument in waking up the institutional Church to its lack of responsiveness of the will of God.[25]

In a recent check on three homophile congregations in the New York City area, I found that a sizable number, perhaps even a majority, of the large groups in attendance at Sunday services were believing Catholics or former Catholics. Most of those interviewed expressed a strong desire to return to the practice of their faith, but only on condition that the Church would be willing to accept them as they are.

Among Catholic homophiles the most important attempt to date to establish such a community—one that accepts the homosexual as he is and yet remains within the Catholic Church community—is that of Dignity, whose newsletter is quoted above. In their original statement of Position and Purpose, the members of Dignity give the following description of themselves:

A. We believe that Gay Catholics are members of Christ's Mystical Body, numbered among the people of God. We have an inherent dignity because God created us, Christ died for us, and the Holy Spirit sanctified us in Baptism, making us his temple, and the channel through which the love of God might become visible. Because of this, it is our right, our privilege and our duty to live the sacramental life of the Church, so that we might become more powerful instruments of God's love working among all people.

B. We believe that Gays can express their sexuality in a manner that is consonant with Christ's teaching. We believe that all sexuality should be exercised in an ethically responsible and unselfish way.

C. As members of DIGNITY we wish to promote the cause of the Gay community. To do this, we must accept our responsibility to the Church, to Society and to individual Gay Catholics:

1. To the Church: to work for the development of its sexual

theology and for the acceptance of Gays as full and equal members of Christ.

2. To Society: to work for justice and social acceptance through education and legal reform.

3. To individual Gays: to reinforce their self-acceptance and their sense of dignity, and to aid them in becoming more active members of Church and Society.

D. Dignity is organized to unite all Gay Catholics, to develop leadership and to be an instrument through which the Gay Catholic may be heard by the Church and Society. There are four areas of concern:

1. Spiritual Development: We shall strive to achieve Christian maturity through all the means at our disposal, especially the Mass, the sacraments, personal prayer and active love of the neighbor.

2. Education: We wish to inform ourselves in all matters of faith as well as in all that concerns the Gay community so that we may develop the maturity of outlook needed to live fulfilling lives in which sexuality and spirituality are integrated, and to prepare us for service in the Gay community.

3. Social Involvement: As Catholics and as members of Society we shall become involved in those actions that bring the love of Christ to others and provide the basis for social reform.

a. Toward individuals: We wish to live a life of service to others, hoping to render visible the love of Christ and contributing our share to building a community of love.

b. With Gay groups: We wish to work with other Gay groups for the cause of justice to the Gay community and for the promotion of a sense of solidarity.

c. With religious and secular groups: We wish to work with them that they may better understand Gays and recognize present injustices.

4. Social Events: Activities of a social and recreational nature will be provided to promote an atmosphere where friendships can develop and mature, and where the Gay's sense of acceptance and dignity may be strengthened.[26]

The obvious reason why the Church has refused until now to recognize the Catholic homophile community is the persistence of the traditional moral judgment concerning the homosexual. It is my personal belief and hope that the Church will undertake a serious reappraisal of its traditional moral judgment, especially since that judgment rests on extremely debatable grounds both in Scripture and tradition. Further, the potential contribution which the homophile community can make to the human and spiritual development of the human community as a whole is a resource which the Church desperately needs at this point in history.

Moral Norms and the Homosexual

Such an acceptance of the homophile community in no way implies that the Church must drop its divinely imposed task of upholding moral ideals in the area of sexual behavior. Rather, the Church must and should continue to uphold moral ideals for the truly human use of sex. However, it must not continue to confuse these moral ideals with the purely formal element of heterosexuality as such. As Thielicke points out:

> The primary moral problem in sexual relations is not sex within marriage versus sex outside of marriage, or sex within a heterosexual versus sex within a homosexual relationship. The problem is sex as a depersonalizing force versus sex as fulfillment of human relationship. Thus the important question would appear to be whether or not it is possible for the homosexual to achieve a responsible fulfilling relationship.[27]

The same moral norms should be applied in judging the sexual behavior of a true homosexual as we ordinarily apply to heterosexual activity. Negatively, any sexual activity that involves exploitation of another person is unequivocally to be condemned. As a Quaker study puts it:

> This is a concept of wrongdoing that applies to both homosexual

and heterosexual actions and to actions within marriage as well
as outside of it. It condemns as fundamentally immoral every
sexual action that is not, as far as humanly ascertainable, the result of mutual decision. It condemns seduction and even persua-
sion and every instance of coitus which, by reason of disparity
of age or intelligence or emotional condition, cannot be a matter
of mutual responsibility.[28]

From a positive viewpoint the will of God for human sexuality is an ideal state in which sexual activity would be en-
tirely dominated and consecrated by mutual love and devo-
tion. Such an ideal is seldom realized in its fullness even in
heterosexual relationships within marriage. Selfishness is never
completely absent from heterosexual relationships. Yet the inevitable presence of this factor within a sexual relationship
does not lead the Church to condemn it and advise a married
couple to refrain from sexual activity as sinful. Their sex can
be justified insofar as it contributes to the development of a
fulfilling and satisfying relationship based in mutual love.

From a moral viewpoint, however, a further problem exists
concerning the individual's sexual development. Most moralists
argue against moral culpability for a homosexual condition,
since they presuppose that such a condition is the result of an
unconscious psychological process which lies radically outside
the conscious and, therefore, free self-determination of the
individual. I am inclined to agree with this position. The majority of homosexuals seem to experience their condition as a
given over which they have little or no conscious control. However, insofar as freedom and an element of conscious choice
can or does enter into an individual's sexual orientation, to
what extent is he morally free to choose a homosexual orientation?

Michael Buckley and other traditionalists believe that there
is an element of choice and freedom in the sexual orientation
of most homosexuals. They argue that insofar as human free-

dom and choice can enter into and influence one's sexual development, one is morally obliged to choose heterosexuality. Some moderns would argue, on the other hand, that insofar as freedom enters into the sexual identity, the ideal is not to choose either homosexual or heterosexual orientation, but to remain potentially bisexual in order to avoid the restrictions that necessarily accompany a choice of identity.

In contrast to both these positions, I believe that the moralist should emphasize the moral insight of Kierkegaard: The truly ethical question is not so much *what* you choose as it is *that* you choose. One begins to be ethical only after one has made a real commitment. Kierkegaard's point is that God as absolute value is never given to us as an object of choice. Rather, we can encounter the absolute only by committing ourselves absolutely to the relative. St. John states forcibly that "God is love, and if any man loves he knows God." If true Christian and human love can exist equally in a homosexual or in a heterosexual context, then there is no a priori base for a moral choice between these contexts.

However, the real moral choice concerns committing or failing to commit ourselves to a fellow human being. The person who would deliberately remain at the immature stage of ambiguity in his sexual preferences will tend to remain uncommitted in his personal relationships. The failure to make a true commitment to another human person is, perhaps, the essential moral failing in all sexual relations, whether heterosexual or homosexual. We have already explored the prudential reasons for choosing a heterosexual orientation whenever that remains an open possibility. But the prior moral question is one of the quality of the commitment one makes to a fellow human person. Insofar as the subjective ambiguity of one's sexual preferences is used as a means of rationalizing a failure to commit oneself with fidelity in a genuine sexual love relationship, that ambiguity should be considered an amoral state.

However, for one who enters actively into sexual relationships to maintain such an ambiguity in order to avoid commitment could represent an immoral choice.

As we have seen, there is a considerable body of evidence— the Hooker and Shofield studies, for example—that many homosexuals have avoided the trap of promiscuity and depersonalized sex by entering into a mature homosexual relationship with one partner with the intention of fidelity and mutual support. By means of this relationship they have not only escaped promiscuity in their relationship but have grown as human beings; they have learned to integrate their sexual impulses in a positive way into their personality, so that these impulses become no longer a negative, compulsive, and destructive force, but an instrument within their control for the expression of human love. Catholic homosexuals are well aware of their need for God's grace in order to remain faithful to their commitment and in order to grow in their power to express unselfish love. This is the motivation behind their seeking a liturgy of friendship. The Quaker committee, after a long study of homosexuality, drew the conclusion: "Surely it is the nature and quality of a relation that matters; one must not judge it by its outer appearance but its inner worth. Homosexual affection can be as selfless as heterosexual affection, and, therefore, we cannot see that it is in some way morally worse."[29]

Norman Pittenger, the noted Anglican theologian, believes that the primary spiritual problem that faces the Christian homosexual is his or her need, in Tillich's words, "to accept divine acceptance":

> I should add that the homosexual who decided for a long relationship, as he may hope a life-long one, with another of his own sex, is almost certainly doing the very best thing that is open to him. Nor do I have the slightest doubt that God can and does bless the relationship. The basic question here for the homosexual is whether he will let the human love which to him

is so wonderful find its grounding in the divine Love, in God himself. That it *is* so grounded I take to be a matter of fact, so far as Christian faith is concerned. . . .

But to *let* it be grounded, to allow it to be consciously realized and felt, requires human surrender. So I should ask the homosexual, "Will you *let* God bless you? Will you *let* him work in your life and in your friend's life and in the life you share together?"

God made men to become true lovers; he wants them to be the best they can possibly be. To acknowledge this and try to base one's existence and one's relationships on it, in full responsibility, gives that existence and that relationship a meaning and a dignity which otherwise they cannot have.[30]

The Positive Role of the Christian Homosexual Community

The recent militancy of the homosexual liberation movement has posed a new moral dilemma for the individual Christian homosexual. The "Gay Liberation" movement has placed a strong stress on the moral and social duty of the homosexual to "come out of the closet," to stop hiding his condition by conforming to an alien heterosexual image, and to proclaim himself publicly as a homosexual. Such a step, they claim, is necessary in order that the individual may win the freedom which will enable him to commit himself to public work for the social and political liberation of his homosexual brothers and sisters.

The Christian homosexual frequently finds this stress particularly challenging, since it gives concrete expression to the central Christian value of self-sacrificing love for one's neighbor, especially the outcast and the oppressed. He is usually well aware that it is most often selfish fear and a desire to escape personal humiliation, suffering, and loss that motivates his desire to hide his identity.

One presiding officer in the Gay Activist Alliance confided to me that it was the Christian value of committing oneself to help one's fellow human beings and the Christian hope of being able to derive strength for others from one's own suffering and pain that originally led him into a religious order as a novice, and which eventually led him to take an active role in the Gay Liberation movement. A surprising number of those Catholics who are active in the movement come from a similar religious background. The call to an open and honest proclamation of one's own homosexuality and a commitment to work for the good of the homosexual community strikes a deep, resonant chord in the spirit of every committed Christian homosexual.

Such a public commitment has its obvious advantages; for it frequently carries with it a deep experience of joyful liberation, a freedom from the deceit and hypocrisy which so frequently poison the lives of homosexuals. From their sociological survey of thousands of male homosexuals in three countries Weinberg and Williams conclude that, all other things being equal, coming out of the closet can be psychologically healthier than trying to hide one's sexual orientation. Looking at the question from a moral viewpoint, it can be said that if one has a clear choice between two courses of action one of which is probably healthier than the other, one has a clear moral obligation to choose that course which offers the greatest promise of health. But "coming out" carries with it many very serious difficulties as well. Perhaps the central problem is the consequences of a public proclamation for one's family and friends. Most Christian homosexuals have found it necessary to continue to conceal their sexual identity from their family because they are convinced that knowledge of their condition would cause their family untold pain and sorrow and no good would come of such a revelation. However, a recent *New York Times* article noted that among young homosexuals many are revealing their condition to their immediate family and finding acceptance and understanding. Perhaps the most success-

ful and imaginative apostolate to the homosexual community
undertaken by a priest is the effort of one priest in the Brooklyn diocese to organize the families of young homosexuals,
who have been through the difficulties of accepting a homosexual son or daughter, so that they can help other parents
through to acceptance and understanding.

Certainly, the Church should accept as one of its pastoral
aims to help create such a relationship within the family. As
we noted earlier, no greater disservice can be done to the family of a homosexual than to continue to insist on the unproven
assumption that somehow the homosexuality of their child is
due to a moral failing in the parental relationship. For such
an insistence effectively blocks the possibility of a young homosexual being able to be open with his parents in a spirit of
love and understanding. Rather, stress should be placed on
the obligation parents are under to accept a homosexual son
or daughter with understanding and love. As we have already
said, whenever one has the good fortune, in counseling, to encounter a psychologically healthy homosexual, aware of his
own dignity and his capacity to love and be loved, one can
be almost certain that his parents, whatever their disappointment over his condition, have responded to him with true acceptance and love.

Unquestionably, the ideal situation that should exist between the individual and his family is one of openness and
acceptance. But there is no easy solution that can be given be-
forehand to any individual faced with the problem of revealing himself to his family. I shall never forget the grief of a
young man who, because he loved his parents very much and
wished to spare them the grief of learning of his condition,
had chosen to live in a distant city, when he received the following revelation at his father's funeral: before his death his
father confided to a friend that he could not understand why

his son had moved away, and felt that perhaps his son did not appreciate how much he loved him.

Two factors must be weighed by each individual faced with this problem of self-revelation to his or her family. The first is the degree to which the individual can foresee whether or not his parents can bring themselves to genuinely accept him with knowledge of his condition. Secondly, the individual must estimate his own psychological strength. Will he be able to accept whatever happens in a spirit of understanding and compassion, and not react with bitterness and disillusionment?

Granting acceptance within one's family and by one's friends, there still remains the further challenge of deciding to play an active, public role for homosexual liberation. There surely are those among the Christian homosexual community whom God is calling to play a prophetic role in society in this regard. But here as in any prophetic role, such as the martyrs of old or the peacemakers of recent times, there must be a prudential and prayerful testing of spirits. The prophet must always pay a terrible price of personal suffering in order to bring about a true change in social attitudes. Before any individual commits himself to a public role, he must determine as best he can ahead of time what could be the worst things that could befall him: loss of his job, contempt and even hatred from society, personal injury, even prison, etc. And he must attempt to predetermine as best he can, based in his past experience and his self-knowledge, whether or not he has the interior strength to pass through such ordeals and come out a better human being because of them, and not cynical or bitter, a broken human being.

The prophetic function is essential if there is to be any advance in justice and charity toward the homosexual in the human community. Yet it can only be fulfilled under ordinary circumstances by someone who has the support of a loving community. Consequently a Christian community, such as Dignity, is essential to give the necessary human and spiritual support.

Another function which the Christian homosexual community can perform is that of providing models. Homosexuals, especially the young, have a desperate need of models of what it means to live out a full human life as a homosexual. They especially need models of how to integrate spiritual and moral values into their life-style. One of the primary functions of social structure is to provide models for the young. The same social climate which forces homosexuals to hide their identity also effectively prevents any such role from being played within the ordinary structures of society. Consequently, there is need of a community within which the homosexual may encounter and come to know those who are sincerely trying to live such a human life with dignity.

One area in which the homosexual has a special need of both models and special counseling is in the realm of interpersonal relationships. The Church recognizes the need young heterosexuals have of special help in this area. Therefore, she has provided such services as pre-Cana and Cana conferences, and many forms of marriage and family counseling. A homosexual couple is even more desperately in need of such services. It is only within the context of a homosexual community that they could be provided.

The Accusation of Sexism

Richard McCormick, a moral theologian, states very clearly the primary objection of some moralists to a recognition by the Church of a homosexual community as such. He accepts the judgment of Francis Touchet:

> The homophile organizations (such as the Gay Liberation Front, Gay Activist Alliance, The American Church) ignore the prime

focus on persons for a chosen focus on sexual preference and in doing so are guilty of an enslaving sexism.[31]

Consequently, McCormick views such organizations as jeopardizing an acceptance of the homosexual and as their own worst enemy because of their "monochromatic view." It must be conceded that any homophile organization that factually does focus exclusively on sexual preference and ignores the prime focus on persons would do a serious disservice to the homosexual, since he is frequently tempted to exaggerate the role that sexuality plays in life.

But I seriously question Touchet's assertion that such is the "chosen focus" of the organizations he names. First of all, the need for such homosexual organizations is based on the fact that the choice of a sexual focus and a sexual qualification of membership has already been made by society at large. There is at least an implicit, if not explicit, condition in most social institutions that one must be heterosexual in order to be accepted and fully participate in that institution. Nor is the Church exempt from such an exclusive condition. On the contrary, by viewing heterosexuality as the divine will and as "the ideal and the normal," as McCormick himself states, the Church has already set up a sexual condition which excludes the genuine homosexual from full participation in its structures. It makes no more sense to accuse the homosexual of an a priori chosen sexual focus than it would to accuse the blacks of a chosen skin-pigmentation focus or women's groups of a chosen biological focus. In each of these cases, as with homophile groups, the purpose of the group is to allow a focus on the person over against a denial of that focus by society at large.

Further, the fact is that the organizations Touchet mentions, although they do exist for those who are homosexually oriented, do not focus on sexuality as such. The Gay Liberation Front and the Gay Activist Alliance both are concerned with the transcendent personalist goals of justice and equality. The American Church has as its objective to make spiritual values and a life of worship available to the homosexual. Obviously, if the homosexual existed in an ideal human society where true justice and love were present there would be no need for such organizations. And, as we have seen, homophile organizations tend to see themselves as interim communities; their ideal is true integration of the homosexual as an equal into human society. But until the time that such an ideal can begin to be realized they have an essential role to play in its acquisition.

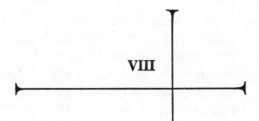

VIII

Conclusion: Justice, the Church, and the Homosexual

The 1971 International Synod of Catholic bishops issued a statement, *Justice in the World,* in which they emphasized that action for justice is an essential dimension of the Church's mission in the world:

> Action on behalf of justice and participation in the transformation of the world fully appears to us as a constitutive dimension of the preaching of the Gospel, or, in other words, of the Church's mission for the redemption of the human race and its liberation from every oppressive situation.[1]

A conclusion that would appear to follow from this study is that one of the "oppressive situations" which call for action on behalf of justice is the situation of the homosexual. Although in all likelihood the bishops of the world did not have the homosexual as such explicitly in mind when they drew up their statement, yet much of what they had to say about justice applies to the situation of the homosexual.

The bishops recognize that the message of love in the Gospel implies an absolute demand for the recognition of the dignity and rights of one's neighbor. "Justice attains its inner fullness in love. Because every man is truly a visible image of the invisible God and a brother of Christ, the Christian finds in every man God himself and God's absolute demand for justice and love."[2] The message of the Christian homosexual community is that for the most part such a recognition has not been extended to the homosexual within the Christian community. The Synod insisted that, if the Church is to be credible when it speaks to the world, it first must be just itself in its own life. This practice of justice in its own life must begin with an unequivocal acknowledgment of, and respect for, the rights of all persons who together are the Church. "Within the Church rights must be preserved. No one should be deprived of his ordinary rights because he is associated with the Church in one way or another."[3] Again, the Christian homosexual believes that he has been deprived of his rights as a condition for his continued association with the Church. Among these rights are the right of association and the right to be heard in decisions which affect his life.

The Synod acknowledges that frequently Christians simply do not see structured social injustices as sin. Consequently, they feel no obligation to do anything about them. As one commentary on the Synod document notes, we tend to ignore the fact that most of our personal choices occur within a societal framework which conditions, controls, and channels personal choice. So powerful and persuasive are these social situations that people frequently are not even conscious of their existence. They are inclined to see "laws of nature and of God" in what are purely human creations.[4] As a consequence Church members tend not to accept responsibility for the social structures which embody and make operational attitudes of prejudice and blindness. The homosexual community is inclined to see the unconscious univocal heterosexual structuring of society precisely as a human creation mistakenly accepted as the law of nature and of God which results in prejudice and blindness. Discrimination against women, the Synod acknowledges, has been structured unconsciously into the life and operation of the Church. As Archbishop Leo Byrne commented:

> Women are not to be excluded from any service of the Church, if the exclusion stems from questionable interpretation of Scripture, prejudice or blind adherence to merely human traditions that may have been rooted in the social position of woman in other times.[5]

If the findings of this study are correct, then the Church's attitude toward homosexuals is another example of structured social injustice, equally based in questionable interpretations of Scripture, prejudice, and blind adherence to merely human traditions, traditions which have been falsely interpreted as the law of nature and of God. In fact, as we have seen, it is the same age-old tradition of male control, domination, and oppression of woman which underlies the oppression of the homosexual.

When social structures oppress human dignity and freedom and maintain situations of gross inequality, the persons who share life within these situations also share responsibility for allowing them to continue. There is, then, a need and an obligation to undertake a process of consciousness-raising, whereby these injustices and the structures that support them can be identified. "Education . . . will awaken a critical sense, which will lead us to reflect on the society in which we live and on its values; it will make men ready to renounce these values when they cease to promote justice for all men."[6] Frequently in the past certain unjust social structures—slavery, for example—were defended and maintained because certain social values, such as stability and economic prosperity, were mistakenly understood as linked to the maintenance of these structures. In more recent times the inferior status of woman is defended and maintained for the same reasons. But once the Church arrived at a clear consciousness that these supposed values were being maintained only by the perpetuation of essential injustice and disregard for the dignity and rights of certain of its members, it was obliged in conscience to reject these structures and do everything in its power to bring about a more just social order. The primary argument for the continued oppression of the homosexual is the belief, in reality unfounded, that the stability of the family and the moral health of society demand such an oppression. There is good reason to believe, as we have seen, that just the opposite is the case. It is the present oppressive situation which helps undermine the family structure by limiting the heterosexual to narrow and dehumanizing stereotypes and also by frequently forcing the homosexual into marriage. As Cardinal Carberry commented: "Help must be provided for the various minority peoples so that each group will not only acquire for itself that dignity and status in social life which is its due, but also will be able to enrich the other groups by the contribution of the riches that are inherent in its own character and culture."[7] Although Cardinal Carberry in all probability did not have the homosexual minority in mind, there is, as we have seen, a potential enrichment of society as a whole which would result from the homosexual community being helped to play its role in society in a constructive way.

All members of the Church are called on by the Synod to be prophetic in championing the rights of individuals and groups that are treated unjustly and in calling for an end to all forms of injustice. Participation by persons in the discourse which affects their lives and destinies is recognized by the Synod as a basic right and human need. There is a special need to implement that right within the Church itself so that everyone can be heard in a spirit of dialogue. The Synod made the point that the action of the Church is to be directed above all "to those men who because of various forms of oppression and because of the present character of Society are silent, indeed voiceless, victims of injustice."⁸ This is certainly the situation of the Christian homosexual within the Church itself. Consequently, the Church authorities should recognize the same right for the Christian homosexual minority that the Synod proclaims for all minority groups, the right of association and the right to enter into dialogue with authorities and the rest of the community. All too often in the past, the Church and its moral theologians have made a priori statements concerning the morality and life-style of homosexuals without any serious effort at dialogue. In this area especially the words of Cardinal Dearden apply: "We must freely acknowledge that the Church must learn and not merely teach what is required in justice."⁹ Homosexuals within the Church have an obligation, and therefore a right, to organize and attempt to enter into dialogue with Church authorities. Church authorities in turn should show an example in terms of just behavior toward the homosexual minority by displaying an active willingness to hear, to enter dialogue, and to seek ways to resolve whatever injustice becomes clear as a result of dialogue. It is only by means of such a dialogue that the Church can attain true consciousness of the injustices which the homosexual suffers and a real process can begin of separating the wheat from the chaff, the true implications of Christian faith and morality for the homosexual from the misunderstandings and prejudices of the past.

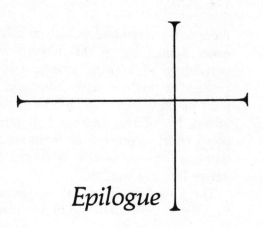

Epilogue

Three major theses have traditionally dominated the thinking of moral theologians concerning homosexuality. As we have seen, each one of these theses is open to serious question today. In fact, in each case a new understanding of human sexuality and new evidence concerning the life-style of homosexuals seem to support the contradictory thesis.

The first thesis is the traditional belief that the homosexual condition, and subsequently all homosexual activity, is contrary to the will of God. It was God's intention that all humans should be heterosexual. Consequently, we must search for an etiological explanation of the homosexual condition in sin, whether that be original sin, the sin of the parents, or the personal sin of the individual homosexual.

In contradiction to that thesis, we have argued that the homosexual condition is according to the will of God. God so created humans that their sexuality is not determined by their biology. We are born male and female; we become men or women by a process of education that is unconscious for the most part. We now know from psychology that a homosexual phase is a normal phase of the sexual maturing process; that

193

there is a homosexual as well as a heterosexual component in every human being; that always and everywhere a certain percentage of humans emerge from that complex learning process as predominantly homosexually oriented through no fault of their own. We have seen that in the light of today's knowledge of the Bible and of human sexuality, the traditional effort to prove from Scripture and from the natural law that such an orientation is contrary to the will of God no longer has any validity.

The second traditional thesis sprang from the first. Granted that the homosexual condition is contrary to the will of God, the presence of the homosexual in the human community is a menace to that community, and especially a threat to the values of the family. Consequently, everything should be done to isolate and "cure" the individual homosexual; or, failing that, to deny him or her any right to exercise their sexuality.

Over against that thesis we have proposed ·that granted the homosexual is here according to God's will, God had a divine purpose in so creating human nature that a certain percentage of human beings are homosexual. In other words, homosexuals frequently are endowed with special gifts and a divinely appointed task in the construction of a truly human society. Rather than being a menace to the community in general and the family in particular, they have an important role to play in preserving and strengthening values such as interpersonal relations between the sexes and the development of a moral understanding of human sexuality outside the procreative context; values which are essential to the community and the family.

Finally, moral theologians have traditionally believed that the love which unites two homosexuals in a sexual union is a sinful love which separates them from the love of God and places them in danger of eternal damnation. In recent times theologians have attempted to buttress that judgment with so-called empirical evidence coming from certain psychiatrists to the effect that homosexuals are necessarily mentally ill and all homosexual relationships are humanly destructive.

In contrast to that thesis—and perhaps most controversially—I have posed the thesis that there is the possibility of morally good homosexual relationships and that the love which unites the partners in such a relationship, rather than alienating them from God, can be judged as uniting them more closely with God and as mediating God's presence in our world. The new empirical evidence in support of this thesis is, first of all, the psychological evidence that homosexuality is not necessarily an illness and the empirical evidence that there are many homosexual couples in stable unions whose relationship provides the context for mutual growth and fulfillment. Further, there is evidence of the work of the Spirit bringing into existence believing communities of homosexuals who in a spirit of love and forgiveness are seeking dialogue with that same institutional Church which so often in the past and in recent times has been their persecutor.

I have been asked frequently to clarify further what I mean by "ethically responsible homosexual relationships." Obviously what I mean first of all is to distinguish between a homosexual relationship that is built on selfishness and mutual destructiveness and a relationship that is unselfish and constructive. I agree with Thielicke that the primary moral problem in sexual relationships is sex as a depersonalizing force versus sex as a fulfillment of human relationship.

Further, I do maintain that there are objective values and moral norms governing the constructive human use of sexuality. These norms are objective in the sense that they are intimately related to the nature of the human person as such, and thus have universal validity wherever there is growth toward the fullness of human personality. There are the negative norms involving a relationship based on the value of justice—e.g., any sexual relationship that involves exploitation of another person is immoral. The positive norms are based on the value of interpersonal love as the ideal human context for sexual expression. These positive norms must be derived from the concept of the human person as an end in himself, or herself, and from the necessary conditions of possibility for a genuine interpersonal love relationship. Among these conditions I personally believe are such norms as mutuality, fidelity, unselfishness, etc.

I hope in the near future to explore a new ethical understanding of human sexuality as a form of human play—where play is understood as any action which has its meaning in itself in the here-and-now; that is to say, an action that is end-in-itself, just as the person is end-in-himself or herself.

Beyond these general principles I believe it is impossible for me at this point to define more clearly or to lay down a priori what the nature of an "ethically responsible homosexual relationship" should be. This is a task which necessarily must be reserved to the Christian homosexual community and its own communal discernment of its experience. As John Milhaven said in his recent letter concerning my manuscript to the *National Catholic Reporter*:

> If anything is clear about human sexuality, it is that Christians today are experiencing values in it that were generally unknown to the traditional Christian. . . . Can one presume that there are no similar developments in homosexual experience? Can one expound the "meaning of human sexuality" without having a clear idea of what actually takes place in homosexual love in our culture? Can one pronounce moral judgments on homosexual behavior without ever taking a long, unblinking look at the actual experience of homosexual love in our times?
>
> May more and more of the real experiences of Christian homosexuals find through brave men . . . expression in the forum of the Church. It is up to the Church, all of us, to speak and listen and gradually, carefully, form a helpful consensus on this agonizing question.
>
> We will be doing only what the Christian community has done on troubling issues many times in the past.

Notes

NOTES TO THE INTRODUCTION

1. For a recent restatement of these traditional aims cf. "Principles to Guide Confessors in Questions of Homosexuality," *Bishops' Committee on Pastoral Research and Practice,* National Conference of Catholic Bishops, 1973.

2. *A New Catechism: Catholic Faith for Adults* (London: Search Press, 1967), p. 384.

3. Vol. 212, no. 1 (June 1971).

4. Vol. 98, no. 5.

5. "The Church and the Homosexual," *National Catholic Reporter,* vol. 9, no. 38.

6. Among John Harvey's more recent publications are the following: "The Controversy Concerning the Psychology and Morality of Homosexuality," *American Ecclesiastical Review,* vol. 167, no. 9 (November 1973), 602–629; "Attitudes of a Catholic Priest Towards Homosexuality," *Bulletin of the National Guild of Catholic Psychiatrists,* December 1972, pp. 52–58.

7. *The Blondelian Synthesis: A Study of the Influence of German Philosophical Sources on Blondel's Method and Thought;* vol. 1 in the series "Studies in the History of Christian Thought," ed. Heiko Oberman (Leyden, Holland: Brill, 1966).

8. *Proceedings of the Jesuit Philosophical Association,* 1968. I call attention particularly to the responses to the questions and critical comments at the end of the article.

9. *Conscience: Its Freedom and Limitation* (New York: Fordham University Press, 1971), pp. 107–124.

10. Vol. 33, no. 3 (September 1972), 503–530.

11. Cf. also the critical response of my peers Charles Curran (below, pp. 29f.) and John Milhaven (below, note 169 to Part 1).

12. Washington, D.C.: Catholic University Press.

13. An example of this new data is to be found in the sociological study of Drs. Martin S. Weinberg and Colin J. Williams, *Male Homosexuals: Their Problems and Adaptations* (New York: Oxford University Press, 1974).

NOTES TO PART 1

1. Notre Dame, Ind.: Notre Dame University Press, pp. 184–219.

2. *Homiletic and Pastoral Review* 70 (1970), 667–677, 747–758, 828–836.

3. Curran, *Catholic Moral Theology in Dialogue,* p. 217.

4. Ibid., pp. 216–217.

5. Ibid., pp. 185–186.

6. Ibid., p. 219.

7. Ibid.

8. I believe the most radical difference in the approach to moral evaluation of homosexuality between Charles Curran and myself is that, as I understand it, he is still working within a natural law context which allows him to make such theoretical distinctions as "objective" versus "subjective" sin. Whereas in contrast I am approaching the problem from a personalist philosophical perspective where such a distinction would be meaningless.

9. "Homo/Hetero: The Struggle for Sexual Identity," *Harper's,* September 1970.

10. Curran, *Catholic Moral Theology in Dialogue,* p. 217.

11. *Homosexual Oppression and Liberation* (London: Allen Lane, 1974), p. 4.

12. Compiled by Harold I. Lief, *Medical Aspects of Human Sexuality* (Baltimore: Williams & Wilkins, 1975), p. 176. Cf. also Eugene C. Kennedy, *The New Sexuality: Myths, Fables and Hang-Ups* (Garden City, N.Y.: Doubleday, 1972), pp. 177–178.

13. Curran, *Catholic Moral Theology in Dialogue,* pp. 214–216.

14. McNeill, "The Christian Male Homosexual," pp. 828–836.

15. Curran, *Catholic Moral Theology in Dialogue,* pp. 214–216.

16. Ibid.

17. *Homosexuality and the Western Christian Tradition* (London: Longmans, 1955), pp. 1–28.

18. Curran, *Catholic Moral Theology in Dialogue,* p. 189.

19. Helmut Thielicke, *The Ethics of Sex* (Cambridge: James Clarke, 1967), pp. 227–284.

20. Curran, *Catholic Moral Theology in Dialogue,* p. 189.

21. Ibid.

22. *The Documents of Vatican II,* ed. Walter M. Abbott, S.J. (London: Geoffrey Chapman, 1966).

23. Alfred Kinsey et al., "Homosexual Outlet," *The Homosexual Dialectic* (Englewood Cliffs, N.J.: Prentice-Hall, 1972), pp. 3–30.

24. *Homosexuality and the Western Christian Tradition,* p. X.

25. Donald W. Cory, *The Homosexual in America* (New York: Julian Press, 1951), p. 8.

26. *A New Catechism: Catholic Faith for Adults* (New York: Herder, 1967), pp. 384–385.

27. *Counseling the Invert* (Milwaukee: Bruce, 1960), p. 17.

28. Quoted by Altman, *Homosexual Oppression and Liberation,* p. 20.

29. *Homosexuality and the Western Christian Tradition,* p. 10.

30. Ibid., "Sodom and Gomorrah," pp. 1–28.

31. "Sodomy," *Encyclopedia of Religion and Ethics,* vol. 11, p. 672a.

32. *Metamorph.* viii.625ff.

33. Unless otherwise indicated all scriptural excerpts are taken from *The Complete Bible: An American Translation,* trans. J. M. Powis Smith and Edgar J. Goodspeed (Chicago: University of Chicago Press, 1939).

34. There are six references to the sin of the Sodomites in the

Old Testament: Gen. 13:3; 18:20; Jer. 23:19; Ezek. 16:49–50; Wis. 10:8; 19:13–14; Eccles. 16:8.

35. *The World of the Judges* (Englewood Cliffs, N.J.: Prentice-Hall, 1965), p. 168.

36. Notre Dame, Ind.: Notre Dame University Press, 1968, p. 143.

37. Ibid., p. 199.

38. Ibid., p. 199.

39. A special word of gratitude is in order here to Dr. John Boswell of Yale University, whose unpublished research on the Pauline texts is one of the principal sources of the materials I use here. Dr. Boswell tells me that he has revised some of the conclusions in his original manuscript. His book, which will be a major scholarly contribution, hopefully will be published soon.

40. Bailey, *Homosexuality and the Western Christian Tradition*, p. 39. The recently revised version has changed the translation.

41. "Die Dualistische Struktur der Paulinischen Teugend und Lasterkataloge," *Die Teugend und Lasterkataloge im Neuen Testament* (Berlin, 1959), pp. 108–114.

42. Contrary to the popular misconception that homosexuals are effeminate, the majority of male homosexuals prefer manliness in themselves and in their partners. Further, most transvestites and males with effeminate characteristics are as a matter of fact heterosexually inclined.

43. "Thus it was natural, your majesty, for men to imitate all these things, and to become adulterers and mad after man (*arrenomaneîs*), and perpetrators of other frightful deeds, in imitation of their gods (ix).

"Is it at all possible, then, for a god to be an adulterer, or a corrupter of boys (*androbátēs*), or a parricide? . . . If, indeed, the laws are just, then their gods are altogether unjust, since they commit crimes, internecine murders, sorcery, adultery, theft and (*arsenokoitías*)." *Arsenokoitías* is linked by the context with *arrenomaneîs* in such a way that it seems likely that the author implies much more than merely homosexual practices.

44. *Patrologia Graeca*, ed. J. P. Migne, 88, 1893c (hereafter cited as *PG*): "And an inquiry concerning *arsenokoitías:* There are

three kinds of this. For it is one thing to suffer it from someone else, doing which is less serious. It is yet another thing to do it to someone else, more serious than to suffer it. Another thing to suffer it from someone and do it to someone, which is even more serious than the two types already mentioned."

45. *PG* 83, 1895a: "And many even practice the vice of *arsenokoitías* with their wives."

46. Unpublished manuscript cited above.

47. Robert W. Wood, "Homosexual Behavior in the Bible," *Homophile Studies: One Institute Quarterly*, Winter 1962.

48. J. Edgar Brun, "Old Testament History and the Development of a Sexual Ethic," *The New Morality* (Philadelphia: Westminster).

49. Ibid.

50. Herman A. M. J. M. van de Spijker, *Die Gleichgeschlechlicke Zuneigung* (Freiberg, 1968), pp. 94–95.

51. "A Brief for a New Homosexual Ethics," *The Same Sex* (Philadelphia: Pilgrim, 1969), pp. 67–70.

52. H. L. Strack and P. Billerbeck, *Kommentar zum Neuen Testament aus Talmud und Midrash* 2, 373.

53. Curran, *Catholic Moral Theology in Dialogue*, p. 202.

54. *Church Dogmatics: A Selection*, ed. G. W. Bromily (New York: Harper, 1962), p. 200.

55. T. C. DeKruijf, *The Bible on Sexuality* (DePere, Wis.: St. Norbert's Abbey Press, 1966), p. 53. DeKruijf himself does not refer to the possibility of homosexual love. The author is responsible for the application of DeKruijf's insight to the question of homosexuality.

56. Ibid., pp. 67–69.

57. Ibid., p. 69. Part of the reason why marriage is no longer stressed is, as we shall see, eschatological: the expectation of the imminent end of the world and the second coming of Christ.

58. *Revised Standard Version and the Apocrypha*, copyrighted 1957 by the Division of Christian Education, National Council of the Churches of Christ in the U.S.A.

59. Ibid.

60. Evelyn Hooker, "Foundations for Christian Family Policy,"

New York Council of Churches Report (New York, 1961). Also
Michael Shofield, *Sociological Aspects of Homosexuality* (Boston:
Little, Brown).

61. Once again I call the attention of my readers to both the
majority opinion of theologians and the tradition underlying the
Church's official teaching on sexual ethics, namely that there is a
biblical norm for the ethical use of sexuality according to God's
will and that norm is heterosexuality. My conclusion here is in
conflict with that majority opinion and tradition. Consequently it
should be carefully and critically appraised by the reader. The
value of my conclusions does not rest on any authority but on the
value of the reasoning and evidence that I have provided and
also on the extent to which my conclusions receive confirmation
in the experience of the reader.

62. Curran, *Catholic Moral Theology in Dialogue*, p. 202.

63. Ibid., p. 203.

64. Citations are derived from Bailey's "Homosexual Interpretation of the Sin of Sodom," *Homosexuality and the Western
Christian Tradition*, pp. 9–28.

65. W. R. Morfill and R. H. Charles, *The Book of the Secrets of
Enoch* (Oxford, 1896), pp. XXIII-XXIV and 49, note.

66. *De Abrahamo* xxvi.134–136; in Philo's *Works*, trans. F. H.
Colson, Loeb Classical Library (London: Heinemann), vol, 6,
pp. 69–71.

67. *Gen. Rabbah* 50.7.

68. *Paed.* iii.8.

69. *Ad pop. Antioch. hom.* xix.7.

70. *De civ. Dei* xvi.30.

71. *Const. apost.* vii.2. For other references to the sin of Sodom
cf. Ephraim the Syrian, *Hymns on the Faith* i.26; *Hymns on the
Nativity* i; John Chrysostom, *In Heli. et vid.* iv; *De perf. carit.* vii;
In Matt. hom. xlii.3; *In epist. ad Rom.* iv; *In epist. ad Thess.* viii.3;
In epist. ad Tit. hom. v.4; Augustine, *De mend.* vii (10); *Contra
mend.* ix (20,22); xvii (34); *Conf.* iii.15; *De fid., spe et carit.* lxxx;
Gregory, *Dial.* iv.37; *Moral.* xiv.19; *Const. apost.* vi.27–28; Tertul-
lian (?), *Sodoma*.

72. Van de Spijker, *Die Gleichgeschlechlicke Zuneigung*, pp. 100–101.

73. *Inst.* iv; xviii.4. The research materials for the development of law are derived from Bailey's *Homosexuality and the Western Christian Tradition*.

74. *Cod. Theod.* ix; vii.3 (*Cod. Just.* ix; ix.31), *The Theodosian Code*, trans. Clyde Pharr (Princeton: Princeton University Press, 1952), pp. 231–232.

75. *The Age of Justinian and Theodora* (London, 1921), vol. 1, p. 121.

76. *Cod. Theod.* ix; vii.6; cf. Pharr, *The Theodosian Code*, p. 232.

77. *Cod. Justin.* nov. 77.

78. *Cod. Justin.* nov. 141.

79. Ed. J. Chitty (London, 1826), vol. 4, p. 215.

80. *Conc. Illib.* 71.

81. *Conc. Ancyr.* 16, 17. Cf. C. H. Turner, *Ecclesiae Occidentales Monumenta Juris Antiquissima* (Oxford, 1909), vol. 11, p. 19. For the influence of this council on future enactments cf. *Capit. Aquisgran* (789) 48, Mansi xviib, col. 230; *Capit. Carol. mag.* 48, Mansi xviib, col. 710; *Capit. Carol. mag. et Ludovic.* 82, Mansi xviib, col. 839; *Canones Isaac episc. Lingonen* 4, 11, Mansi xviib, col. 1259; *Conc. Paris* (829) 1, 34, Mansi xiv, col. 560.

82. *Epist.* ccxvii (*ad Amphiloch.*), can. 62.

83. *Epist. canonica* iv.

84. *Conc. Tolitan.* 16, 3, Mansi xii, col. 71.

85. *Conc. Neapol.* 8, Mansi xxi, cols. 261–264.

86. Cf. *Synod. constit. Odo. episc. Paris* (ca. 1196) 4, 5 (the pope or the bishop), Mansi xxiii, col. 678; *Conc. Prov. Fritzlar* (1246) 4 (bishop), Mansi xxiii, col. 726; *Stat. syn. eccl. Leod.* (1287) 4 (bishop), Mansi xxiv, col. 891; *Conc. Ramense.* (1408), Mansi xxvi, col. 1073.

87. *Patrologia Latina*, ed. J. P. Migne, 145, col. 161 (hereafter cited as *PL*).

88. Mansi xix, cols. 685–686.

89. *Chron.* in Rolls series, ed. W. Stubbs (London, 1879), vol. 2, under A.D. 1120.

90. Bailey, *Homosexuality and the Western Christian Tradition*, pp. 135–144.

91. Louis Crompton, "Module No. 10; Gay Genocide: From Leviticus to Hitler," *Salvatorian Justice and Peace Commission: Gay Minority Task Force*. Cf. also Wolfgang Harthauser, "Der Massenmord an Homosexuellen im Dritten Reich," *Der Grosse Tabu*, ed. William S. Schlegel (Munich: Rütten & Leening Verlag, 1967).

92. *The Same Sex*, p. 71.

93. New York, Ballantine, chap. 4, pp. 72ff.

94. Bailey, *Homosexuality and the Western Christian Tradition*, pp. 161–162.

95. *Paed*. 10.

96. *De fac. nat*. 1.6.

97. Bailey, *Homosexuality and the Western Christian Tradition*, p. 164.

98. *Society and the Healthy Homosexual* (London: Colin Smythe, 1975), pp. 1–21.

99. "Homosexuality as a Pastoral Problem," *Theological Studies* 16 (1955), 86–108.

100. Bailey, *Homosexuality and the Western Christian Tradition*, p. 162.

101. *Const. Apost*. vi.11; vi.28.

102. *De pudic*. iv.

103. *In Epist. ad Rom*. iv.

104. *Le Stoicisme des pères de l'église de Clement de Rome à Clement d'Alexandrie* (Paris, 1957), p. 432.

105. Cf. F. Copleston, *A History of Philosophy*, vol. 1, pt. 2 (London: Burns and Oates, 1962), pp. 138ff.

106. *Diogenes Laertius* 7.86ff.

107. Marcus Aurelius, *Med*. 5.27.

108. Cf. "Stoicism," *New Catholic Encyclopedia*, 716–721.

109. *Ibid*., p. 720.

110. *Paed*. 1, chap. 13.

111. Marcus Aurelius, *Med*. 7.29.

112. Ibid., 19.

113. Seneca, *Epist*. 120, 14; 65, 16.

114. Aquinas, *Commentary on the Nichomachean Ethics*, trans.
C. I. Litzinger (Chicago: Regnery, 1964), vol. 2, bk. 9, lect. 10,
no. 1896.

115. Von Arnim, *Stoic. Vet. Frag.*, vol. 1, pp. 59–60.

116. Emil Brunner, *The Divine Imperative* (Philadelphia: Westminster, 1947), p. 364.

117. *On the Generation of Animals*, 737a.

118. *The City of God* 14.26. Cf. also *On Marriage and Concupiscence* 2.5.

119. "*De divisione naturae*," *PL* 122, 57c.

120. *Paed.* 2.10; *De concept.* 92.2.

121. *I Apol.* 29.1.

122. *In Evang. Luc.* 17.29.

123. *Summa Theol.* II-II, q. 153, 3.

124. *Summa Theol.* III, q. 32, 4.

125. *Summa Theol.* I, q. 99, 2.

126. *Summa Theol.* I, q. 92, 1.

127. *Summa Theol.* I, q. 98.

128. Cf. Joseph McCaffrey, "Homosexuality, Aquinas and the
Church," *Catholic World*, vol. 212, no. 1 (July 1971).

129. *Summa Theol.* II-II, q. 154, 12, ad 1.

130. *Summa Theol.* I-II, q. 37, 7.

131. Curran, *Catholic Moral Theology in Dialogue*, p. 199.

132. Ibid., p. 204.

133. Ibid.

134. Cf. *Seven Great Encyclicals* (Paramus, N.J.: Paulist Press,
1963), pp. 93–94.

135. Ibid. p. 84.

136. "Pastoral Constitution on the Church in the Modern World
—a Response," *The Documents of Vatican II*, ed. W. Abbott, pp.
314–315. Cf. also "The Pastoral Constitution . . ." no. 50: "Marriage to be sure is not instituted solely for procreation. Rather, its
very nature as an unbreakable compact between persons, and the
welfare of the children, both demand that the mutual love of the
spouses, too, be embodied in a rightly ordered manner, that it
grow and ripen. Therefoie, marriage persists as a whole manner
and communion of life, and maintains its value and indissolubility,

even when offspring are lacking—despite, rather often, the very intense desire of the couple."

137. Søren Kierkegaard, *Fear and Trembling* (Cambridge: James Clarke, 1941), pp. 80–82.

138. Cf. John McNeill, "Freedom and the Future," *Theological Studies*, vol. 33, no. 3 (September 1972), 503–530.

139. *Sex: Thoughts for Contemporary Christians*, ed. Michael Taylor, S. J. (Garden City, N.Y.: Doubleday, 1972), pp. 49–62.

140. For evidence on this point cf. Wainwright Churchill, *Homosexual Behavior Among Males* (New York: Hawthorne, 1967).

141. London, SCM, 1963, p. 136.

142. *Toward a Christian Understanding of Homosexuality* (New York: Association Press, 1966), p. 56.

143. *The Bible on Sexuality*, p. 69.

144. *Catholic Moral Theology in Dialogue*, p. 190.

145. Ibid., p. 192. Cf. also John Giles Milhaven, *Toward a New Catholic Morality* (New York: Doubleday, 1972), pp. 59–63.

146. *Catholic Moral Theology in Dialogue*, p. 193.

147. Ibid.

148. Ibid., p. 203.

149. Ibid.

150. William Simon and John Gagnon, "Homosexuality: The Formation of a Sociological Perspective," *Journal of Health and Sociological Behavior*, vol. 8 (1966), 177–185.

151. Curran, *Catholic Moral Theology in Dialogue*, p. 196.

152. Ibid., p. 203.

153. *Homosexual Oppression and Liberation*, p. 52.

154. New York: Collier, 1956, pp. 1–10.

155. Irving Bieber, *Homosexuality: A Psychoanalytic Study* (New York: Basic Books, 1962), p. 5.

156. Altman, *Homosexual Oppression and Liberation*, pp. 44–46.

157. *Homosexuality: Disease or Way of Life*, p. 4.

158. "Letter to an American Mother," *The Problem of Homosexuality in Modern Society*, ed. Hendrick Riutenbeek (New York: Dutton, 1963), pp. 1–2.

159. *Homosexuality and the Sickness Theory* (San Francisco: The Society for Individual Rights, 1963), p. 4.

160. Cf. Churchill, *Homosexual Behavior Among Males,* pp. 106–122.

161. *Counseling the Invert,* p. 37.

162. *Toward a Christian Understanding of Homosexuality,* p. 52.

163. Churchill, *Homosexual Behavior Among Males,* p. 105.

164. Ibid.

165. *Foundations for Christian Family Policy.*

166. *Toward a Christian Understanding of Homosexuality.*

167. John Milhaven, "Homosexuality and the Christian," *Homiletic and Pastoral Review,* vol. 58, no. 8 (May 1968), 665.

168. Ibid., pp. 667–668.

169. In a recent letter to the editors of the *National Catholic Reporter,* John Milhaven himself announced that in the light of new evidence he rejects his former opinion: "McNeill is right. My original essay had ignored the important evidence he then set forth. In revising my essay for book publication I acknowledged McNeill's argument and evidence. I altered substantially my own position, bringing it closer to his." (Cf. "Repartee," *National Catholic Reporter,* 4 December 1975.)

170. *Homosexuality: Disease or Way of Life,* p. 24.

171. Bieber, *Homosexuality: A Psychoanalytic Study,* pp. 100–150.

172. For a history of causes and cures as they have been pursued through time cf. Arno Karlen's *Sexuality and Homosexuality* (New York: Norton, 1972). For a critical summary of recent "cure" techniques of therapy cf. G. Weinberg, "The Case Against Trying to Convert," *Society and the Healthy Homosexual,* pp. 41–48.

173. Gerald C. Davison, President of the Association for Advancement of Behavior Therapy, recently rejected the use of aversion therapy as a means of "curing" the psychic condition of homosexuality. On the contrary, Mr. Davison reports, "the vast majority of behavior therapists would indeed help their homosexual clients adjust more satisfactorily to a permanent homosexual identity."

174. *The Manufacture of Madness* (New York: Harper, 1970). Reprinted as "The Product Conversion: From Heresy to Illness," in *The Homosexual Dialectic,* ed. J. McCaffrey (New Jersey, 1972), pp. 101–120.

175. *The Homosexual Dialectic*, p. 108.
176. Ibid., p. 109.
177. Irving Bieber, *New York Times*, 15 September 1967, p. 27.
178. *Must You Conform?* (New York: Holt, 1956), pp. 32–33.
179. Pp. 3–21.
180. Ibid., Preface.

NOTES TO PART 2

1. "An Open Letter on Homosexuality," *Sex: Thoughts for Contemporary Christians*, ed. Michael Taylor (Garden City, N.Y.: Doubleday, 1972), p. 211.
2. Ibid., p. 212.
3. *New York Times*, 25 February 1972, p. 41.
4. *New York Times*, 25 February 1972, p. 41.
5. Nappey, "An Open Letter on Homosexuality."
6. Brun, *The New Morality.*
7. *The New Sexuality: Myths, Fables and Hang-Ups*, pp. 179–180.
8. Nappey, "An Open Letter on Homosexuality," pp. 217–218.
9. Ibid., pp. 210 and 218.
10. Kennedy, *The New Sexuality: Myths, Fables and Hang-Ups*, p. 179.
11. C. G. Jung, *The Collected Works,* trans. R. F. C. Hull (London: Routledge, 1959), vol. 9, pt. 1, pp. 86–87.
12. *Letters to a Young Poet*, trans. M. D. Herter (New York: Norton, 1962), pp. 58–59.
13. Louis Crompton, "Module No. 10: Gay Genocide: From Leviticus to Hitler," *Salvatorian Justice and Peace Commission: Gay Minority Task Force.* Cf. also Wolfgang Harthauser, "Der Massenmord an Homosexuellen im Dritten Reich," *Der Tabu*, ed. Schlegel, pp. 17–37.
14. Altman, *Homosexual Oppression and Liberation*, pp. 74–75.
15. *The Ethics of Sex*, pp. 227–284.
16. *Psychology Today*, vol. 8, no. 10 (March 1975), 27–33.
17. Pp. 72ff.
18. *Collected Works*, vol. 9, p. 86.

NOTES TO PART 3

1. *Ethics in a Christian Context*, p. 137.
2. In order to be accepted by a majority of the delegates, the final resolution had to be reworded to eliminate reference to a homosexual community as such. Consequently, it read "Christian ministry to the homosexual." Many delegates felt that the Church could not proceed to recognize the existence of a homosexual community and retain its traditional moral judgment on homosexual activities. Thus the only ministry possible would be one to individuals as such.
3. Pp. 12–13.
4. New York: Sheed and Ward, 1957, p. 100.
5. New York: Dutton, 1960, p. 10.
6. *Counseling the Invert*, pp. 258–259.
7. Richard F. Hettlinger, *Living with Sex: The Student's Dilemma* (New York: Seabury, 1966), pp. 94–112.
8. *Homosexuality* (London, 1960), p. 47.
9. Donald W. Cory and John LeRoy, *The Homosexual and His Society* (New York: Citadel, 1963), pp. 104–105.
10. *Morality and the Homosexual* (London: Lamb's, 1959), p. 19.
11. Cavanaugh, *Counseling the Invert*, p. 262.
12. Ibid., p. 263.
13. Ibid., p. 262.
14. *Nobody Knows My Name* (London: Corgi, 1969).
15. *Counseling the Catholic*, p. 102.
16. *Toward a Christian Understanding of Homosexuality*, p. 88.
17. *A Minority: A Report on the Life of the Male Homosexual in Great Britain*, p. 28.
18. West, *Homosexuality*, p. 51.
19. "Sublimation and the Homosexual," *Pastoral Psychology*, vol. 2, no. 18 (November 1951).
20. "Clerical and Lay Value Systems," *Modern Society*, vol. 12, no. 4 (August 1969).
21. Cf. O'Neil and Donovan, *Sexuality and Moral Responsibility* (Washington, D.C.: Catholic University Press): "Sin is properly

sin because it opposes the will of God. But this 'will of God' is neither arbitrary nor vindictive. Following the thought of Aquinas we see that the divine will is really identical with the true good of man. . . . In this context it is worthwhile to repeat our basic premise, good morality and good psychology cannot be in conflict. There is no contradiction between the supernatural good of man and his ethical good."

22. *The Ethics of Sex*, p. 105.

23. *Dignity: A Monthly Newsletter for Catholic Homophiles and Concerned Heterophiles*, vol. 3, no. 4 (May 5, 1972).

24. Martin S. Weinberg and Colin J. Williams, *Male Homosexuals: Their Problems and Adaptations* (New York: Oxford University Press, 1974).

25. *Journal of the New York Mission of the Metropolitan Community Church*, vol. 1, no. 1 (March 1972).

26. Information about Dignity can be obtained by writing to *Dignity*, 755 Boylston St., Rm. 413, Boston, Mass. 02116.

27. *The Ethics of Sex*, pp. 281–287.

28. *Toward a Quaker View of Sex*, ed. Alastair Huron (London, 1963).

29. That there can be a morally good sexual relationship between two homosexuals who love each other is my personal conviction. Once again I call attention of my readers to the fact that this conviction contradicts the traditional teaching of the Church in this matter. It is not my intention to attempt to supplant the magisterium but, rather, to invite a public debate and discussion of this issue in the hope that the Church will listen and reconsider its position. In the meantime the only authority my conviction has is the intrinsic value of the reasoning and evidence that I can bring to its support.

30. *Time for Consent* (London: SCM, 1970), pp. 122–123.

31. Richard A. McCormick, "Notes on Moral Theology," *Theological Studies*, vol. 33, no. 1 (March 1972), 112–113. Cf. also Francis H. Touchet, "A View from the Other Side of the Garden," *Listening* (Winter 1971), pp. 42–48.

NOTES TO THE CONCLUSION

1. Synod Document, 9 December 1971. Translated in *Catholic Mind,* vol. 70, no. 1261 (March 1972), 53.

2. Ibid., p. 57.

3. Ibid., p. 59.

4. "The Quest for Justice: Guidelines to a Creative Response by American Catholics to the 1971 Synod Statement, 'Justice in the World'." Issued by the Jesuit Center of Concern, 25 June 1972.

5. Synod, 22 October 1971. Quoted in "The Quest for Justice," p. 5.

6. *Justice in the World,* p. 60.

7. John Cardinal Carberry, Synod, 21 October 1971. Quoted in "The Quest for Justice," p. 11.

8. *Justice in the World,* p. 55.

9. John Cardinal Dearden, Synod, 21 October 1971. Quoted in "The Quest for Justice," p. 4.